Whitehead's View of Reality

Charles Hartshorne
Creighton Peden

The Pilgrim Press
New York

Library of Congress Cataloging in Publication Data

Hartshorne, Charles, 1897-
  Whitehead's view of reality.

  Includes bibliographical references.
  1. Whitehead, Alfred North, 1861-1947.   2. Whitehead, Alfred North, 1861-1947 — Theology.   3. Philosophical theology.   4. Methodology.   I. Peden, Creighton,
1935-   joint author.   II. Title.
B1674.W354H38   210   80-23532
ISBN 0-8298-0381-5 (pbk.)

Quotations from Alfred North Whitehead, *The Function of Reason* are Copyright 1929, © 1957 by Princeton University Press, pp. 5-69. Reprinted by permission of Princeton University Press. Other extensive Whitehead quotations are: Reprinted with permission of Macmillan Publishing Company, Inc. from *Process and Reality* by Alfred North Whitehead. Copyright 1929 by Macmillan Publishing Company, Inc., renewed 1957 by Evelyn Whitehead. Reprinted with permission of Macmillan Publishing Company, Inc. from *Modes of Thought* by Alfred North Whitehead. Copyright 1938 by Macmillan Publishing Company, Inc., renewed 1966 by T. North Whitehead.

The Pilgrim Press, 132 West 31 Street, New York, New York 10001

Preface

At various transitional stages in human development, particular philosophers have been of crucial importance. Alfred North Whitehead is such a philosopher. It is hoped that this volume will assist and encourage the serious student to an indepth consideration of Whitehead's thought. In it we present an analysis of the historical context in which Whitehead's philosophy develops and then present an exposition of various aspects of his position.

In our society today there is a continuing dialog concerning the appropriate use of language, including pronouns referring to God. While we are sensitive to the issues in this dialog, the language employed has been selected because it seems appropriate to the historical context of Whitehead's thought.

Although there are many students and colleagues to whom we are indebted for critical discussion, we would like especially to express our appreciation to Carolyn Vickers for her efforts in manuscript preparation.

Charles Hartshorne
Creighton Peden

TABLE OF CONTENTS

Whitehead in Historical Context
Charles Hartshorne

Whitehead's Philosophy: An Exposition
Creighton Peden

Whitehead in Historical Context

by

Charles Hartshorne

The Basic Categories

What Whitehead called speculative philosophy, the central or noncontingent core of which he sometimes called metaphysics, is a difficult enterprise; and at most only a few crucially important individuals occur in it in a century. Plato and Leibniz were outstanding examples in the past, and in the hundred years ending in 1970 I personally take the most important to have been Peirce, Bergson, and Whitehead. Whitehead was deeply influenced by Plato and to some extent by Leibniz and Bergson but came to know about Peirce as philosopher too late to be influenced directly by him. Like Whitehead, Peirce, and Leibniz, Plato took mathematics to be an important aid in philosophizing. Plato's Academy was supposed to be open only to those who had studied geometry. Whitehead wrote the article on geometry for the great Eleventh Edition of the Britannica. Leibniz, Peirce, and Whitehead, as few others in the history of philosophy, combined intensive work and competence in mathematics, formal logic, physics, and speculative philosophy. They were well acquainted with the history of science and philosophy, as well as with the intellectual situation in their own time.

Bergson was not a mathematician or formal logician, though he did a year's work in mathematics at the Ecole Normale Superieure and won a prize in that subject. His theory of intuition rationalized his lack of high competence in rigorous reasoning. Whitehead thought, as many others have, that this lack somewhat limited Bergson's achievement. In any case Whitehead took Bergson's views into account, and one can claim that he assimilated much of what was best in them.

There are philosophers important for speculative philosophy who are not important in speculative philosophy. These are the critics of speculative systems who scarcely have a system of their own, the skeptics or agnostics who point to weaknesses in systems and, in this way, enable the system-makers to do a better job. Among these relatively nonspeculative thinkers, Hume, Kant, Russell, William James, and Wittgenstein have been important. Except apparently for Wittgenstein, Whitehead certainly considered these thinkers with some care.

The line between system-makers and critics is not sharp. Of the writers just listed, at least four--Hume, Kant, Russell, and James--took some steps into metaphysics. But Hume's metaphysical doctrine is an extreme pluralism summed up by the words, "What is distinguishable is separable," where "separable" means that either of two distinguished items might conceivably exist or occur without the other. Thus, if we distinguish two events, a and b, occurring in that order, then a might conceivably have occurred though b did not follow, and b might have occurred though a had not preceded it. This doctrine of mutual independence makes causal dependence of events on previous conditions a mystery. (Russell repeats Hume in this respect and his philosophy, apart from niceties in formal logic, adds little to the Humean paradox.) Hume also takes a metaphysical position in defending causal determinism. This not only does not follow from his pluralism but seems incongruous with it. True, Hume thought that empirical science had established determinism. However, as Kant rightly argued, no such concept as absolute and universal causal order could be justified by mere observation.

Whitehead, like Peirce, seems to have begun his philosophizing as a student of Kant but doubtless saw that Kant's ideas of science, mathematics, and logic were partly antiquated by intellectual progress after Kant's time. Kant was not himself a mathematician or formal logician, though he did make some contributions to natural science. Kant's agnosticism, his rejection of much of what had been metaphysics, was combined not only with an acceptance of determinism but also with a concept that Hume tried to show was fallacious, that of "substance"--meaning the idea of a thing which changes through time and yet remains in an absolute sense the "same" reality. Kant did not exactly accept Hume's pluralism; but he avoided it only by attributing causal dependence and order, also substantiality, not to the things given in our experience but to our human way of experiencing them. So the order we know is to be taken not as that of things as they are apart from us, but only as the order of our experiences themselves. We know ordered appearances not ordered realities. And we have no theoretical evidence of the existence of God or human freedom, even though for ethical reasons we need to believe in them.

Whitehead accepts from Hume his critique of substance (or of absolute genetic identity) and on this point disagrees somewhat with Kant. But he agrees with Kant that absolute pluralism is a mistaken doctrine, not, however, because our minds force the given into some causal order but because causal dependence is in the things we experience, quite apart from our experiencing them. Moreover, he holds (and there may be an

3

influence of James here) that Hume and Kant are both wrong in absolutizing causal order in the deterministic fashion. All events have necessary conditions in previous events, but they do not have strictly "sufficient" conditions if that means conditions strictly determining what then happens. For Whitehead, as for Bergson and James (also Peirce, but Whitehead did not know about his views until his own were fully formed), there is always at least a bit of freedom or uncertainty in what a given situation will produce as its effect. The past is settled and present action must "conform" to it; but always there is more than one possible way of achieving this conformation. On the higher levels we call this indeterminacy freedom. Peirce's word for it was "spontaneity," Bergson's and Whitehead's was "creativity." Berdyaev, exiled Russian thinker, had a similar view and used the same word (but also "freedom"). Dewey too believed that indeterminacy was found in nature apart from humanity.

On one issue Whitehead agrees with all the great metaphysicians mentioned in the first paragraph of this essay. Plato, Leibniz, Peirce, Bergson, all believed that the explanation of matter was to be sought in mind, not that of mind in matter. Of the four, Plato was least clear on this point, but he did hold that mind (or "soul") was "self-moved" and the source of all motion or change. For Leibniz what we call matter is merely mind in low-grade forms and in various kinds, individual instances of each kind (atoms, cells, etc.) occurring in large numbers. These instances are insignificant taken one by one and are therefore perceived by us only in masses, like a swarm of bees seen at a distance. Peirce followed Leibniz in this analysis and so did Bergson. Whitehead is in this tradition, which he developed and clarified. He regarded the notion of mere matter, dead and without feeling or thought, as an empty abstraction, and one the usefulness of which in science had been steadily diminishing in recent decades. On this issue three great mathematician-logician-philosophers agree. There is also some agreement on this topic between the three Western philosophers and the Buddhist tradition in Asia. A Buddhist slogan was "mind only."

On the question of substance, or absolute identity through change, Peirce is somewhat unclear, and so, I find, is Bergson, while Leibniz was the extremest defender of strict substantial identity. Whitehead, Hume, and the Buddhists agree that, strictly speaking, a so-called substance is a new concrete reality each moment; but it is Whitehead who, in my judgment, does the best job of retaining aspects of truth in our commonsense notions of individual things and persons. One can read into Plato a view somewhat like Whitehead's, and Bochenski has even hinted (in conversation) that the gulf between Whitehead and Aristotle on this point could easily be exaggerated. The point of Whitehead's rejection of substance in the usual meaning is not that there is no identity through change. There is identity, but it is partial or qualified, not absolute or total.

There is an asymmetry about genetic identity. An adult possesses or carries its childhood with it in a sense in which a child does not carry or possess its adulthood. Identity in its absolute meaning has no such asymmetry. If X simply is Y, then in the same sense Y is X. The rings of a tree enable us to inspect the tree's past, but nothing similarly discloses its future. Memory is the psychical analogue of the tree rings. Remembering is experiencing our past selves. Each of us carries throughout life a mass of mostly unconscious memories, and after early childhood this mass begins to form the central core of our sense of identity. No one else has the same memory mass, and the longer we live the less, proportionately, does each new momentary experience add to the total. It is also true that, even with identical twins, no one else has exactly the same bodily structure, changes in which are mostly small and gradual, especially after early adulthood. Each of us is also the focus of various obligations and expectations coming to us from others, linked to our names or our appearances, and this, too, tells us "who" we are.

People who talk about their "search for identity" or their puzzle about their identity, are expressing in one way the truth that self-identity is not an absolute, simple affair, but a qualified, relative, partial, subtle, and complex one. The relativity is also expressed in other ways. We say we "identify ourselves" with our children or our spouses. We say that someone was "not himself" or herself. We speak of being "born anew." Then there are multiple personalities. And where, in deep sleep, is one's conscious self?

Why is it that we can scarcely recall our infancy as ours? Show a person a picture of an infant boy or an infant girl. Will the person recall having been that boy or girl even if this was in fact the case? The infant had not yet acquired a memory mass sufficiently comparable, in quality and quantity, to the adult one to be recognizable. If "I" means an individual conscious of self, then the infant scarcely had an "I" to be remembered. Is the adult still that infant? There is an enormous difference, like to or greater than the difference, at least in intelligence, between a cow, say, and a normal human adult. It does not make sense to conceive the infant reality as identically the self that now has adult intelligence. For this is to try to conceive the less as containing the more. To say that the adult self simply is the infant self is to insult the former.

5

We can escape from these paradoxes if we admit, with the Buddhists and Whitehead, that concrete actualities are not in last analysis enduring, changing substances but successive momentary states of what are called substances or individuals and if we assign to these successive states or actualities certain relations, neither simply of partial similarity to their predecessors, nor of sheer identity, but of partial, asymmetrical identity with them. I am now the one recalling a childhood, youth, early adulthood, and middle age not recalled, with anything like the same directness, vividness, or completeness, by any other present actuality (other than God). To remember certain past experiences is to be partly constituted by them. So far as remembered they are elements in oneself still. It is quite false to suppose that a Whiteheadian must, in rejecting sheer identity, be asserting total non-identity. Far from it. The past selves are still in the present self. But the present self was not in those past selves. This is the asymmetry.

If individual self-identity is not absolute, neither is the non-identity of the selves of more than one individual. The past selves that have entered into one's present self are not alone those that one recalls as one's own. Every past self that we once experienced enters in also. Nonidentity among individuals is thus as relative as the identity of each. This is precisely why both Buddhism and Whitehead (and those who follow him in this) see great moral and spiritual significance in the non-substance doctrine. It cuts the self-interest account of motivation at its root. There is no absolute enduring self and (at least among neighbors or acquaintances) no absolute non-self either. Almost the entire Western theory of motivation is biased or ambiguous here. "I love myself because I am myself" has been the principle; if I love you who are not I, that is a puzzling, metaphysically ungrounded addition. As the Buddhists all saw, there is no absolute truth in "I am myself" and equally none in "I am not you." Only relatively am I the identical self through change and only relatively am I not my friends and enemies. Any other doctrine is an extreme form of pluralism between individuals and an extreme form of monism between successive states of one individual. What this double extremism really means if taken strictly is exactly the lesson of Leibniz's monadology. He actually tried to believe consistently and wholeheartedly what most individualists only half or confusedly believe. And the view is not credible when put so sharply and unambiguously (or nearly so--for the idea defies complete clarity and consistency).

Consider our relation to the future, our own and that of others. No one who observes people can pretend that in fact they always seek anything like their own long-run advantage. If this were the case only utter stupidity could explain how frequently and obviously they act contrary to their own long-run advantage. People are not that stupid! Love of our long-run good is not automatic, guaranteed by metaphysical identity, any more than is indifference to the good of others. The truth is much more complex and qualified. There is plenty of selfishness, tragically much, partly encouraged no doubt by metaphysical doctrines exaggerating identity and nonidentity! But there is also a good deal of concern for the future of others. And there is plenty of activity motivated neither by self-love nor love of others, in any reasonable sense, but by momentary or short-run feelings of weariness, boredom, desire, hostility, or fear. The subtlety and complexity of the matter fits the Whiteheadian account better than any usual substance theory. What human beings need is not merely to achieve "enlightened self-interest," but to understand that the only reality worthy of our ultimate devotion is neither the one that uniquely goes with or possesses the own body nor the ones that go with the other human bodies but a Reality beyond or inclusive of all of us, something that is immortal whereas we are mortal, and that possesses our past, not in the meager fashion in which our memories, records, and monuments preserve it for us, but fully and entirely. Of this Reality also, as we shall see, Whitehead gives a helpful account.

We must now come closer to certain technicalities of Whitehead's system. These are called "actual entity," "prehension," and "creativity."

An actual entity is a momentary state or single instance of process or becoming. It is unchangeable, for change, in this scheme, is the succession of actual entities, each of which "becomes but does not change." It is a single creation. First it is not, then it is. Creativity refers to becoming, which brings actualities into being rather than changes actualities already there. Becoming is addition, not subtraction, and change is not its final analysis. Here Whitehead departs from Bergson (also from Peirce), who makes change the essence of becoming, while also saying it is creative.

The example of a single actual entity that we come closest to experiencing distinctly is a single human experience, such as comes to be in a small fraction of a second. We know this example most directly in immediate, short-run memory, which is what "introspection" or self-awareness is in this philosophy. Even this primary example is not quite distinctly experienced. Whitehead, like Leibniz, Peirce, and Freud, holds that our introspective power is limited. We experience, feel, sense, intuit, but have only relatively distinct awareness of what, or how, we experience, feel, or intuit.

7

Actual entities other than our own momentary experiences must be conceived by us as analogous to our experiences. The analogy becomes less and less close as we pass from ourselves to other human beings, then to experiences of non-human higher animals, then lower animals, then single cells, animal or vegetable, then molecules, atoms, particles. It is Whitehead's doctrine that, however remote the analogy, it never totally lapses, so long as we make the distinction between single actualities (or individual sequences of them) and collectives, associations, or crowds, of such single entities. Whitehead's "A tree is a democracy" is his metaphorical way of saying that a cell in the tree is the individual that is to be understood by analogy with a human individual, not the whole tree, which is a colony of cells and subcells. Botany seems to support this distinction. The point is that the tree, lacking a nervous system, lacks the unity of action and feeling which many-celled animals have. Aristotle said, wiser even than he knew, that a plant is "like a sleeping man who never wakes up." (He should have said, "Like a person in dreamless sleep.") In such a state the person is not acting or experiencing as one; it is the various cells which are doing whatever is done.

Peirce and Bergson view experiencing as continuous change. In a continuum no definite single parts can be found; for a point or instant is only a conceptual ideal of an infinitely short stretch of the continuum. It belongs to mathematics, not physics or psychology. To have definite single actualities which are the products or instances of creativity, one must hold, with the Buddhists and Whitehead, that becoming is not strictly continuous, though to our fallible, somewhat vague introspection it appears continuous.

The actual entities are the real subjects that experience, perceive, remember, and think. My childhood self did not, and could not now, think my philosophical thoughts. Each new experience means a new actual subject not there before. Elements in it, my childhood selves included, were there before, but not it.

Now that we know what a single actual subject is, we may ask what it is for a subject to experience. The basic form of experience is perception. Whitehead is perhaps the first philosopher to interpret perception throughout as, no less than memory, experience of the past rather than of the present. By the time we see or hear an event in the environment it has already happened. Whitehead generalizes this retrospective structure of perception so that even when we sense or feel happenings in our bodies our feeling comes after the happenings, not simultaneously with them. Events cannot be experienced until they have already happened. An event is an instance of becoming, and until it has effected its becoming there is no definite entity to be experienced. As already remarked, even introspection, inspection of our own experiences, is short-run memory, is retrospective. Thus all awareness of concrete reality is of the past. The awareness itself occurs now, but not that of which it is aware. In temporal structure perception is like memory. I call perception "impersonal memory," awareness of past events other than our own past experiences. Ordinary memory is personal.

Memory and perception, then, are alike in being intuition of previous actualities. Whitehead calls such intuition "physical prehension." "Mental prehension" is the other kind of intuition, and it is the function of thinking, interpreting the physically prehended, and forming an idea of the future and of contemporary actualities. Since only past actualities are now given, the future and the contemporaries must be known from the past. Our past overlaps with that of our contemporaries; to this extent, and so far as there is causal order, we may be able to know what is going on now around us and is likely to occur in the future.

Whitehead's interpretation of mental prehensions, of thinking, is rather too Platonic for my taste. He talks of "eternal objects," which seem a fairly extreme form of Platonic "ideas." I think one can do with a less realistic theory of universals. Whitehead follows the ancient neoplatonists (and, I believe, by implication Plato himself) in holding that the eternal objects or forms are divine ideas, nothing simply by themselves. Our physical (or "hybrid") prehension (almost entirely nonconscious on our part) of God as having these ideas is the key to our acquiring them, but which ideas are eternal in God and which are divinely or humanly acquired as the creative process goes on is a question deserving more careful inquiry than Whitehead ever gives it. He never faces nominalistic arguments (explaining universals by similarities rather than vice versa). I find more cogency in these arguments than Whitehead did.

Creativity Whitehead calls the "category of the ultimate." The other categories are only aspects of what is implied by this one. In each instance of creativity "the many become one, and are increased by one." The act of "becoming one" is termed a "creative synthesis." This synthesis is the ultimate emergence. The "many" going into the synthesis are the previous actualities, the actor or agent is the new "one," the new actuality. This creation is thus self-creation; for an actuality comes to be as a free act. (Language tends to mislead here, as though actor were one thing and act simply another.) The many become one in the sense of being prehended by a single new partly self-determined actuality. The oneness is

9

synthetic but is just as genuine as that of any previous actuality, which was itself such a synthesis, though not of entirely the same "many." The key to creative synthesis is prehension. An actual entity comes to be as a single though complex act of prehending its predecessors, most of them with negligible distinctness. (Indistinctness is a pervasive feature of all prehending save that of God.)

II

Whitehead's Philosophical Theology

If all prehension whatsoever were indistinct, it would be problematic what could be meant by "indistinct," since there would, it seems, be no standard of distinctness. This is indeed one of Whitehead's reasons for introducing God into his system. He had a predecessor at this point, for Spinoza said that "unclear" ideas in us are unclear in comparison with the divine ideas, which are wholly clear. "The truth itself" wrote Whitehead, "is only the way all things are together in the consequent nature of God." The consequent nature is God as prehending the world, rather than simply contemplating his own eternal reality. Physical prehension, being an inherent aspect of creativity, cannot be lacking even in God, for creativity is ultimate. As all creativity is self-creative, though influenced by other previous cases of creativity, God, too, is self-creative, and the divine acts of self-creation are prehendings or emergent syntheses of all that has already occurred in the world or in God. It follows that God is not in every respect immutable or independent; rather the divine reality perpetually enriches itself by prehending new actualities in the world.

To give Whitehead's thought about God its historical setting is a special problem. He knew fairly well what the Church Fathers had had to say on the subject; he was also acquainted with Plato's and Aristotle's ideas of deity, and the views of Descartes, Spinoza, Leibniz, Hume, and Bradley. He had some knowledge of Hindu, Buddhist, and Chinese religious thought. As a son of a Church of England clergyman (and brother of a bishop) he doubtless knew what "God" usually meant to churchgoers and was familiar with the Scriptures. He had done some reading in the anthropology of religion. Beyond this it is hard to know what close philosophical precedents for his thinking he was aware of. And there were such precedents, most of which, I would guess, he knew little or nothing of. Thus he was to a considerable extent on his own in working out an alternative to the standard metaphysical concept of deity as it had prevailed for about 18 centuries, to some extent since Aristotle.

In addition Whitehead, as he once told me, thought that the full elaboration of a philosophical theology was not his pri-

11

mary task, which was to overcome in principle the divorce between natural science (with its bias toward materialism and abstraction from values, including religious values) and the ideals of civilized humanity. He thought that the full working out of the theological aspect could be left to others. (I think he was at that time aware that I was one of the others engaged in that very task.) So we find that, apart from an obscure and clearly provisional chapter in Science and the Modern World, some cryptic remarks here and there in Process and Reality (and a few even more cryptic ones in Religion in the Making, Adventures of Ideas, Modes of Thought, and the much earlier Function of Reason), Whitehead's account of his theology consists only of the not very long though superb final chapter of Process and Reality, with its sublime poetry and partial technical clarity. In my opinion (and--oddly enough-- that of an able young philosopher I know who, when I last was in touch with him, was an agnostic in religion) this essay is the greatest that has been written on the philosophical idea of God "since Plato's Timaeus." And I have heard Whitehead quoted as having said that it was the most important thing he had written. But to fully appreciate it one may need to know more of the historical background than appears in Whitehead's writing and perhaps more than was in his mind.

Classical theism, in outline well known to Whitehead, was in important respects an amazingly definite and persistent element in Western metaphysics. It identified the God of religion with what philosophers sometimes call "the absolute," meaning by "absolute" totally independent of all else, entirely without change, and a sum of all possible perfections--the actuality, without remainder, of all possible real value. God was the world's "unmoved mover" (Aristotle), First Cause, or Creator, in no way influenced by the creatures' existence. Aristotle deduced from the divine unchangeability and independence the conclusion that God does not know or love the individuals in the world. Rather they know and love God. The key to medieval theology, which was for so long an unchallenged standard, remarkably similar in Judaism, Christianity, and Islam, is the attempt to retain Aristotle's denial that God is influenced or in any way changed by what occurs in the world, while rejecting the Aristotelian deduction that this means God does not know worldly occurrences. Rather God knows and indeed loves creatures, though without being moved by them. In ordinary language to be "moved" by the joy or sorrow of another creature is to sympathize with that creature, to love it, but for medieval theology there is no theological analogy for this. And Aquinas says that relations between God and the creatures are "relations for the creatures, but not for God."

12

What the love of God for creatures can be in God if not a relation is, some of us think we see clearly, entirely beyond intelligible account. And Aquinas admits, in agreement with Aristotle, that in all other cases, S knows Y implies S is influenced by Y. Only in application to God does he reverse the relation, to read, Y is influenced by S. Aquinas says that God knows you or me simply in knowing his own eternal and immutable essence, which is the cause of all things, therefore of you and me. In knowing this cause of you and me God ipso facto knows you and me.

It seems perfectly clear that for Aristotle this doctrine would not make sense, any more than it has to many, if not most, modern philosophers. For, if knowledge of something (the divine essence) is knowledge of all things, and the something is eternal and without contingency, then so are all things. (In something necessary and changeless there can be no implication as to any contingent existent and its changes. What the eternal and necessary implies can only be itself eternal and necessary.) Aquinas is trying, in defiance of logic, to have the eternal and necessary include or entail non-eternal and contingent items.

Aquinas's own language makes this clear enough. For he says that the divine essence is the "cause of all possible things," hence of you and me. But you and I are not merely possible things, we are actual things. And if God knows only that we could exist (and no more can be implied by the essence as possibility of things) he does not know that we do exist. The distinction between what could be and what is constitutes the very meaning of the "contingency of the world" of which classical theism made much!

Beginning in the time of Spinoza, philosophers and theologians began to rebel against the doctrine whose acute paradox I have just outlined. I have taken Aquinas as my example; but on the points at issue dozens of others would have served, except that the Thomistic version was at least as explicit and clear as any.

Spinoza's solution to the problem of divine knowledge was to deny the contingency of the world. He strongly hints, at least, that the world in its reality is as necessary and even as unchangeable as God. What human "imagination" takes as change or becoming is really, "from the standpoint of eternity," i.e., the divine standpoint, an immutable array of items each having relations of effect to its predecessors and of cause to its successors, but all eternally definite and determined by the divine essence. Nor is there any ultimate distinction between possible and actual things. All really possible things

13

are, he held, in their time and place, necessarily actual. There is no contingency.

The Spinozistic solution removes the Thomistic paradox but introduces others, including the clear denial of human freedom in any reasonably normal sense. It also violates the "principle of contrast," the logical truth that to say "everything has the predicate p" adds nothing to the mere tautology that everything is something. (The point of terms like "necessary" is that some things are not necessary.) And most theologians have seen that Spinozism is not an acceptable interpretation of the God of religion. If each actual thing has to be actual because of the divine essence, then it is meaningless to say that the essence is independent of actual things. What something necessitates is what it depends upon, could not be without. True, Spinoza could say that God is eternal while ordinary things are actual only in their time and place; still, by hypothesis, God could not be without them as in that time and place, and this is dependence if anything is.

A little before Spinoza was born a neglected theologian had proposed a very different solution to the central paradox of classical theism. Although a wholly eternal and necessary being cannot know or love the contingent and changeable, there is no reason why a being that is eternal and necessary in its essence should not have changeable accidents, nonnecessary qualities, as it is aware of contingent occurrences in the world. There is no logical rule that says a being eternal and necessary in some respects (constituting its essence, or what makes it always itself) cannot also be temporal and contingent in other respects, constituting its accidents.

The whole point of speaking of an individual's "essence" is the contrast between this and the accidental qualities of the individual. If I happen to see a certain insect, does my being myself depend on this circumstance? We do not ordinarily assume so. Still more relevant, if I make a certain decision tomorrow, does my being myself require that decision, so that any other decision would have to be made by someone else? In that case what becomes of individual freedom? After all, my being myself goes back to what I was at, or before, or soon after birth, and this was dependent on my parents or on God. Is everything I ever do in effect decided as soon as I come to exist? Then in a real sense I decide nothing and am but a wheel in the cosmic machinery.

The first theologians to see the foregoing issue sharply were the Socinians, beginning with Fausto Socinus of Italy. His disciples in Poland and Transylvania carried on and developed the tradition. They took the idea of human decision-mak-

14

ing seriously and rejected the notion that divine omnipotence determines human decisions. Not God but we decide what we do. They saw that this has implications for divine knowledge. God can know that you or I decide to do X only if we do so decide. If we decide to do Y instead of X, then that is what God knows us as deciding. Thus in determining how to act we determine something of God's knowledge. Moreover, God cannot know eternally how we decide, for our decisions do not exist eternally; until a decision is made there is no such thing for God or anyone to know. Thus there must be a temporal aspect of God's knowing. He comes to know actions only as and after they come to be. Hence the immutability of God requires qualification. In thinking in this way the Socinians were very serious people who risked and incurred persecution for their beliefs. They said what they meant and they meant what they said. They knew quite well that they were breaking with a venerable and very formidable tradition. And, some of us believe, they were quite right in doing so.

To the obvious objection that Socinianism "limits" God's knowledge and is incompatible with the divine cognitive perfection or "omniscience," the Socinians had a definite and clear reply. It was that perfect knowledge knows things correctly; but, if decisions do not exist eternally, a knowledge which had them as items in an eternal--meaning timeless or unchangeable--reality would know them as they are not, that is falsely. A not-yet-made decision is no definite entity, but a more or less indefinite one. To know it as that is to know it correctly. God knows definite (past) actions as they are, definite entities, and God knows partly indefinite, not yet determined (future) actions as they are, i.e., in just the indefiniteness which belongs to them. So Socinianism does not limit God's knowledge; rather it alone avoids implying error in that knowledge.

If this reasoning has been refuted I do not know by whom. The astonishing fact is that it was not refuted but ignored or dogmatically dismissed by every important later theologian and philosopher who was presented in standard histories of philosophy or encyclopedias down to the present century. To this very day one cannot find the Socinian view of the partial mutability of God referred to in standard reference works. I regard this as a revealing instance of how false it is that the basic possibilities for speculative philosophy and theology have been exhausted long ago by the well-known figures reported upon in the histories and compendia of knowledge. The French movement called existentialism rests essentially upon this false supposition, as one can see by reading Sartre or Camus. They call existence "absurd," largely on the ground that there is no escape from the dilemma: either omnipotent divine power settles everything and so is responsible for every evil as well as every good and we human beings have no genuine freedom, or we have freedom and there is no God, at least none worth worshipping. It is precisely the Socinian God that is worth worshipping, and that is the one most scholars know nothing about.

After the persecuted Socinians had been reduced to a small remnant in Hungary, views having something in common with theirs were held by Schelling and the psychologist Fechner in Germany, J. Lequier in France, J. Ward, E.S. Brightman, W.P. Montague, W.E. Hocking, and a number of other writers in England and the United States. Whitehead seems to have known something of Schelling but probably not much. He may have known something of Ward's view, rather inferior to Socinus's in clarity, and he may have known that his Harvard colleague W.E. Hocking believed that there is an open future for God in basically the Socinian sense. Probably he did not know about Socinus's, Fechner's, or Lequier's treatment of the issue. The critics of Whitehead have been mostly ignorant of Whitehead's chief anticipators. Another anticipator was Peirce, whose view of God was known, if at all, too late to influence Whitehead, or most of his critics. Peirce's theology was more hinted at than worked out by him.

Some of the writers discussed in the previous paragraph made an important step beyond Socinianism. They generalized the idea of creaturely freedom (as decision-making not causally determined) so that in principle it applies to creatures generally, not just to human beings. The latter have freedom on a higher, more conscious level, but every truly individual or singular creature (not a mere aggregate or aspect of individuals) has at least some minimal kind or degree of the power of settling the otherwise unsettled, deciding the otherwise undecided or indeterminate. This is quite clearly Peirce's view, and also, as I interpret him, Fechner's.

On one point Lequier marked a real advance. Like the Socinians, he is extremely lucid in denying that God either makes or in his eternal aspect knows our actions, and he explicitly asserts that we produce changes in God by these actions. We "make a spot in the absolute" is his phrase for this. More accurately, God is not merely or exclusively absolute or independent but is also relative and dependent. But Lequier also says that in making our decisions we to a certain extent make ourselves. "Thou (God) hast created me creator of myself." Since this ever partly new myself becomes an item in divine cognition, the individual creates something in God. So here we have definite anticipation of the view that a creature is not merely divinely created but is also in some degree self-created and, via this self-creation, is in some degree creative of the

16

divine reality also. I believe that Peirce would have been open to conviction on these points, although he perhaps did not quite arrive at them. He did strongly suggest that God was not simply immutable but somehow increased in content with the world process, each individual of which acted "spontaneously," by which he meant undetermined (though influenced) by past events, and he nowhere asserts that events are fully determined by God.

One more step and we come closer still to Whitehead's view. If the worldly individuals are self-created as well as creative of those who know them (especially God as knowing them fully), what about God? Is he merely creative of, and partly created by, others, or is he also self-created? Unless divine self creation is affirmed, the system is incomplete or inconsistent. (Without some analogy between creature and creator there is no human meaning for theological terms.) It happens that the affirmation of divine self-creation was actually made by two poets of long ago: Ikhnaton of Egypt c. 1000 B.C. and Nezahualcoyotl of Mexico before the Spanish conquest. "With thine own hands fashioning thyself" was Ikhnaton's formula concerning his sun-god, while the Mexican poet (in translation into English via Spanish) wrote, "The creator of all things is creator of himself." It is likely enough that Whitehead did not know even the Egyptian case, and surely not the Mexican. So here, too, he had to do his own thinking, with little definite support from predecessors.

In Whitehead all the foregoing elements come together and have their place in a great system, in some ways the greatest of systems. God for Whitehead is not entirely independent, even of the least of the creatures, nor is any single creature a wholly self-determining, self-creative power. And God is in some aspects creature as well as creator, and is self-creative.

The last point is not stated in so many words but follows manifestly from the "ultimate" category of creativity and the statement that God is the supreme exemplification of the categories, not a mere exception to them. Creativity is always self-creative or free; it is the creative synthesis constituting an actuality, and this self-making is presupposition for any influence upon other actualities. God is both nontemporal and "in a sense temporal," "always moving on" or "in flux."

For this philosophy, God is not the actualization of all possible perfections and it is logically impossible that there should be such an actualization; for possible values are in part mutually incompatible. God cannot have me making decisions I might have made but did not make. The classical concept of perfection lacks coherent sense. Kant suspected this but failed to revise his idea of God to take the point into account. Since possible values are inexhaustible by actuality, there can be no reason for becoming ever to reach a last stage, and this is one aspect of the very rationale of becoming: why there should be anything besides mere immutable being. At last philosophy gives a reason for becoming, the lack of any such reason having been a scandal in its history.

God as classically conceived does not simply happen not to exist. No such being could exist, and its nonexistence is no cause for grief. It was an incoherent idea and the combination of it with the belief that our existence has a meaning (adds something to the value of reality) was a further incoherence. All possible value as fully actualized is not only not a valid concept but it makes nonsense, absurdity in Camus's word, of our existence and the worldly process as such. The problem of evil in classical form is an additional absurdity. One can hardly blame existentialists for their reaction to such a tradition. But, alas, they did not know that there was another theological tradition, by no means open to the same objections.

That God depends for some qualities on the creatures follows easily from the traditional belief that God knows and loves the creatures. Whitehead's view of knowledge is on this point Aristotelian just where classical theism was flatly incompatible with Aristotelian principles. Knowledge rests on prehension, intuitive or cognitive grasp of actualities which do not prehend. The prehended actualities are presuppositions of the particular prehension, not vice versa. God does not make an actuality by prehending it, any more than we do. The divine creative influence upon my present act is not a consequence of the divine prehension of the act, but rather of the divine prehension of the previous situation out of which my act arises. God interprets that previous situation in such a way as to give me my "initial subjective aim," out of which I and I alone create my final or fully concrete subjective aim. Only then can God prehend what I have created.

All this fits perfectly what Lequier says about the same topic. God waits, says Lequier, to see what you or I may decide.

Really it is strange that the point just made was not seen all along in theology. The classical idea deprived worldly existence of all value for God. The worldly process merely reiterated God's eternal plan. It had no reason for being. The entire process throughout time was nothing but a single eternally known complex superfact into which nothing new could ever come. This was an infinitely undramatic, unbeautiful conception. But then Western thought has been crude in its aesthetic understanding more or less throughout. In this respect, too, Whitehead gives us much to be grateful for. The cosmic drama as he depicts it really is that, even for God. The outcome is not in detail foretold, primordially stale and devoid of the unexpected, but is ever fresh and partly new. Our little adventure is included in the "adventure of the universe as one," or as the besouled cosmos.

The importance of each actuality being divinely prehended is that in this way the actuality achieves "objective immortality," enters into a living treasure house where no longer "moth and rust doth corrupt and thieves break through and steal." And so--without positing a survival of death into some miraculous heaven or hell, either as a disembodied (and violently unnatural) soul or as a (not clearly less unnatural) soul with a numerically totally distinct body, or one assembled out of some of the same atoms in a manner entirely unconnected with any known natural laws -- we deprive death of its fundamental threat, which is that what was a living, beautiful actuality becomes a heap of low-level atoms and molecules or a mass of low forms of life. The concrete actualities are the momentary experiences and these will "live forevermore" in the Life of all lives. We will not go on to new joys, nor will our friends; but the joys we have created in ourselves and one another can never be less than they have been. For divine perceptual prehensions, unlike ours, are fully adequate to their objects, and what in God corresponds to personal memory in us (the other basic kind of prehension) is similarly perfect.

For me this form of immortality is existentially sufficient. I do not feel in the least cheated by it. Our friends will never be less than they have been, for themselves or for us, and they will be infinitely more than they could be merely for themselves or for us. (For only God can vividly intuit an entire career with full awareness of each detail and its beauty.) In this way egocentricity can in principle be overcome. Each moment's experience is an offering to the future, inclusively to the divine future which cherishes all achieved value forevermore.

Classical theism cannot give us this hope of serving a cause infinitely greater than ourselves; for its God derived no benefit from our lives. Atheism cannot give it either; for it is limited to what we can do for posterity, which will little remember us, and our effects upon which are very incompletely predictable--quite apart from the manifest impossibility of knowing that there will always be a human posterity. The idea of objective immortality is an immense advantage of process theology over all its rivals. It seems quite safe to anticipate that people will not soon agree in accepting either of the two rival options. This theology seems equipped for a long future, assuming that human culture is not radically diminished by some terrible catastrophe, brought on by misuse of our human freedom, for example by grossly wasteful use of energy and other resources, overluxurious living, unconscientious sexual reproduction, lack of seriousness, emotional control, and willingness to make sacrifices to reduce injustice and avoid international warfare.

However that may be, we need not see existence as absurd. It is dramatic and attended with risk, but so in principle is any possible existence; for risk is inherent in life and awareness is in principle creative. Death need not be viewed as canceling out any actual achievement of concrete value, and we need not believe that God is torturing us; rather it is we ourselves and other creatures that do this, mostly unintentionally. God's allowing this to happen is the same as his allowing genuine self-active individuals to exist at all. The notion of individuals wholly controlled by a supreme individual or superindividual is mere confusion. To be is to act, to be individual is to act individually. The Superindividual makes a reasonably ordered cosmos of self-acting and therefore more or less precariously interrelated individuals possible and immortalizes their actuality. If this is absurd I must lack some organ for detecting that property. And I am not persuaded that the idea of life itself being essentially absurd is anything more than an intellectual and quite human mistake.

III

Some Unresolved Problems in Whitehead's Theism

Whitehead characterizes God as " an actuality." But he scarcely notices that this makes God analogous, not as in most theologies to a person or individual, but to a single, momentary state or experience of an individual. In Whitehead's system a person is a progressively realized "society," an ordered but only retrospectively definite sequence of actualities. Clearly, Whitehead does not mean that God is like a single member of such a sequence. In that case there would be a succession of deities! Moreover, actual entities do not change, they merely become, whereas God changes in the definite sense of acquiring new prehensions as new actualities emerge in the world. It seems obvious that Whitehead, without very clearly recognizing it, is conceiving deity on the model of a society of actualities as much as on the model of a single actuality. I personally would say that the latter analogy is the closer one. Of course with either or any analogy the difference, in some sense infinite, between God and anything else must be kept in mind.

Whitehead is aware that human thought is limited to the kinds of reality encountered in human experience and to what is conceivable by analogy with these kinds. He knows perfectly well that describing God as "the fellow sufferer who understands" is employing analogical language. He knows, too, that the explication of prehension as "feeling of (others') feeling" implies an analogy between our emotional life and the inner quality of actualities generally. Hence in talking of God as feeling our feelings (literally sympathizing with them) he is being consistent. (Berdyaev and the English theologian Garvie --also Origen long ago-- attributed sympathy in this sense to God.) I have never been able myself to see that it makes sense to speak of God knowing our sufferings while in no sense suffering himself. One can know about the sufferings of others by applying an abstract concept called suffering (and even this seems dependent upon having suffered oneself) in referring to the others; still, this is not knowing their sufferings as theirs, as unique to them, and as concrete rather than mere instances of the universal "suffering." But how can a single actuality, which by the definition of an actuality does not change, be "fellow sufferer" to our successive sufferings?

This is one of the ways in which Whitehead's theism is somewhat incompletely worked out. There is, besides the issue between the two analogies referred to, the difficult question of how the temporal aspect Whitehead attributes to God (who is said to be "in a sense temporal") is compatible with the structure of space-time in Einsteinian cosmology, or in Whitehead's cosmology--for he discusses neither scheme in this connection. Quantum theory complicates the matter further. When Whitehead came to Harvard in 1924 he felt obligated to spend his time reading and teaching philosophy, rather than the theoretical physics he had been teaching in London, after teaching mathematics at Cambridge. Consequently his knowledge of physics began to be out of date. Although he had seen Heisenberg's famous article of 1927 on the Uncertainty Principle (I know because a young physicist friend showed it to me and I showed it--or the concluding passages--to Whitehead), there is no evidence that he seriously reacted to the controversy about the "Copenhagen interpretation" of quantum physics, not to mention Bell's Theorem (with the physicist Stapp's "revised Whiteheadian" interpretation of the theorem) and other later discoveries and ideas.

Criticisms of a philosophical system sometimes tell more about the critic than about the system or its maker. Human language is not capable of infinite clarity; always there are ambiguities in a philosophical writing which, resolved in plausible ways, yield absurdities, but perhaps, as the writer intended them to be taken, or as they can be taken, make sense. In Whitehead's use of "perishing," a metaphor taken from Locke, there is ambiguity, as is made clear by the last sentence of PR, "they (actual entities) perish and yet live forevermore." Because of the indistinct or negative prehensions in all nondivine actualities much of the past is lost, no longer available in its fullness, for those actualities. But God surpasses ordinary actualities in this as in other respects, and by the standard of the divine prehensions the partial unreality of the past is an illusion. Also, if actual entities "become but do not change" how can they be deprived of their full reality? This would be a change. And we read in Whitehead's text that for the eminent mode of prehending "there is no loss, no obstruction."

There is some ambiguity concerning the relations of God and creativity. I resolve this as follows. Creativity as "form of forms" or "category of the ultimate" refers to what divine and ordinary creativity (or creative prehending) have in common, namely "decision," making definite what was otherwise partly indefinite, thereby enriching reality. (Beauty depends on definiteness.) But nondivine creativity cannot explain how there can be any order, any limitation to the conflicts and incongruities implicit in the idea of every actuality being self-creative. Given creaturely or nondivine creativity there is bound to be a measure of disorder, conflict, suffering, and on the higher levels some aspects of ethical evil or wickedness. Infallibility, whether ethical or cognitive, is a divine prerogative. But the limitations of nondivine creativity go further. It is already too much to say that nondivine creativity, by itself, can explain even suffering and wickedness. For these phenomena too presuppose some degree of order, some adaptation of actualities to other actualities. Since one cannot adapt to a mere chaos, it begs the question of order to explain it by nondivine adaptation. Hence one of Whitehead's principal reasons for introducing God -- he has at least four, one of which, God as standard of truth, has already been mentioned -- is that deity is precisely that eminent form of creativity which, by virtue of its unique excellence, can influence all other forms and inspire in them the necessary minimum of mutual adaptation without which there could be no universe, no cosmos in which coherent experiences, even painful ones, would be possible. By all adapting to one and the same God, the creatures are enabled to adapt, at least minimally, to one another. No other account of cosmic order can rival this one in simplicity and coherence.

Plato almost said it. All change is explained by "self-moving" soul (Whitehead says, by creatively prehending at least sentient actualities). The lack of complete order is explained by there being many souls. Each is self-active or self-changed, and Plato either meant by this -- though less clearly -- what Whitehead means by creativity, or he meant very little. Plato did see that a multiplicity of souls or creative agents implies indefinitely great if not complete disorder unless there is a supreme soul to "persuade" the many lesser souls to conform to a cosmic plan. They cannot completely fit such a plan for then they would not be self-determined; or, to put it better, the plan cannot be completely definite and detailed. But if there are only the many localized souls, imperfect in their modes of prehension, what would impose any limits on the possible disorder? Whitehead can vastly clarify the self-changing aspect of mind or soul, can explain why much physical reality appears to our sense perceptions as insentient and uncreative, why the nondivine souls need the divine to order them, how it can do this, and why the divine soul needs many nondivine ones to furnish content for its eminent prehending. God would simply be knowing with ideal clarity that very divine knowing--of what? Contrast is essential to beauty, why not the supreme contrast of divine and nondivine?

I have sketched some of the ways in which Whitehead either as he left his work, or with some revisions, brings improved solutions to ancient problems. I hope to publish at least one book, probably two, to show the extent to which this can be claimed.

Process theology is in some respects an unfinished doctrine. This is hardly surprising. Whitehead did not expect to achieve finality. If I am asked, do I know that the process scheme is true? I reply that if "know" means to have absolute, distinct, and infallible consciousness of truth, then I do not know this. But for believing in the view as "something like the truth" (Plato) I see a reasonable case.

My own metaphysics is not entirely the same as Whitehead's by any means. But the points I have chiefly stressed in the foregoing account are largely common to both schemes. I am reasonably content to influence people to give primary attention to Whitehead's thought or to mine. Either way I feel that they will be in better touch with reality than if they rely only on other available offerings of philosophers of our century. In third place I would put Peirce's philosophy, which lacked the benefit of intellectual progress after about 1905, at latest, and also suffered from the undue isolation of Peirce from other thinkers.

The century which produced some terrible things produced a scientist scarcely second in genius and character to any that ever lived, Einstein, and a philosopher who, I incline to say, is similarly second to none, unless it be Plato. To make no use of genius of this order is hardly wise; for it is indeed a rarity. A mathematician sensitive to so many of the values in our culture, so imaginative and inventive in his thinking, so eager to learn from the great minds of the past and the present, so free from any narrow partisanship, religious or irreligious, is one person in hundreds of millions. He can be mistaken, but even his mistakes may be more instructive than most other writers' truths.

Whitehead's Philosophy: An Exposition

by

Creighton Peden

I

INTRODUCTION

Alfred North Whitehead's life and interest can be divided into three periods. The first period extends from childhood until 1914, and is designated as his mathematical period. Philosophy of science becomes the dominant interest in the second period, roughly dated from 1914 to 1924. His appointment as Professor of Philosophy at Harvard marks the beginning of the Metaphysical Period, which lasted until his death in 1947. This division does not imply that all three interests were not active in each stage of his life; rather, it suggests that in Whitehead's life different interests were dominant at different stages.[1] Though our primary attention is devoted to Whitehead's third period, we shall review the development of all three periods.

Whitehead's under-graduate education was historical, classical and scientific. His physical surroundings served as the dominant factor of historical education in his life, for he lived in a community dominated by Roman, Norman and medieval history. His classical education came from the study of Latin, Greek, and classical history, while the study of mathematics developed his scientific interest. At the age of nineteen, Whitehead began his studies at Trinity College, Cambridge. During his student days at Trinity, he never attended a lecture that did not deal with pure or applied mathematics. Yet this educational experience was actually Platonic in form, due to his association with the group known as "The Apostles." It was their custom to meet in the evenings and discuss social and intellectual problems. These discussions demanded a large amount of miscellaneous reading, and it was during this period that he read and re-read Kant.

Moving from student to teacher, Whitehead entered fully into his "mathematical period." His writing during this period indicates this dominant mathematical interest. Whitehead was trying to deal with the mathematical problems raised by the fall of Newtonian physics. In 1903, he discovered that he and his former student, Bertrand Russell, were working on the same problems. They decided to unite their efforts, and this collaboration culminated in the publication of Principia Mathematica. By 1913, Whitehead realized that his interest was turning to philosophy of science and that because of this, it would be necessary to break off his working relationship with Bertrand Russell.

The second period in Whitehead's life is marked primarily by three important works: An Inquiry Concerning the Principles of Natural Knowledge, The Concept of Nature, and The Principle of Relativity. At this stage Whitehead operates from a realistic frame of reference, giving emphasis to the order of nature.2 It is his desire to limit his concentration to this order of nature in order to develop an adequate philosophy of science, and this he was constrained to do by the collapse of the Newtonian philosophy of science.3 The fundamental doctrine developed in this stage is the doctrine of the extensiveness of events.4 Extension is asserted as the ultimate and intrinsic feature of actuality; "the continuity of nature arises from the continuity of extension."5 The majority of Whitehead's metaphysical doctrines are expressed in an under-developed manner in his philosophy of science and are later developed on the basis of his primary doctrine of the extensive nature of events.6 Ivor Leclerc indicates the essential interest of this period and points to its relationship to the later metaphysical period.

> In his early period, especially that covered by Principles of Natural Knowledge and Concept of Nature, Whitehead expressly adopted the scientific procedure of restricting his problems, dealing with only certain aspects of the concrete totality of existence, and thus deliberately abstracting from metaphysical considerations. Although aware that metaphysics was important, and even that his analysis had metaphysical implications, he determined to leave all this out of account. At that time he was fairly conversant with metaphysical thought, but was not himself a metaphysician in the sense of having a metaphysical system of his own. He felt that to admit metaphysical considerations would be obstructive to his endeavour, since traditional metaphysics had proved inadequate to the needs of science and as yet there was nothing to replace it. As opposed to this, he then considered the scientific procedure, of restricting and abstracting, to be both legitimate and fruitful in dealing with the problems of the philosophy of science.7

At the age of sixty-three, when most men are withdrawing from the creative responsibilities of life, Whitehead begins a new profession as a metaphysician. This new endeavour became physically possible by his appointment as Professor of Philosophy at Harvard University. With considerable zest he devoted himself to developing a metaphysical position that would offer a unifying foundation to all disciplines. It had been necessary to deal with the problems of mathematics and physics brought about by the fall of the Newtonian view. An attempt had been made to present a philosophy of science to replace the Newtonian foundation. Whitehead had come to realize that a philosophy of science was not enough; it was also necessary to develop a metaphysical system based on the new scientific insights to replace the fallen metaphysical system of the Newtonian world. The problem of continuity and change, of relating the one and the many, must be dealt with on a metaphysical level. On the basis of the quantum theory and the theory of relativity, Whitehead made "process" the key term for describing the nature of reality. Continuity was no longer seen as pertaining to actuality but, rather, to potentiality.[8] As a metaphysical term, "process" was not limited to the consideration of an all-inclusive concept which served for Whitehead's treatment of "the adventure of ideas" within the "process of history."[9] His metaphysical considerations were based on science, but now science was related to the ongoing problems of the modern world. The problems of religion, of symbolism, of the function of reason, of nature and life, were now all interrelated within the metaphysical system.

Whitehead's greatness is not that he claimed to, or actually did, formulate a metaphysical system which would serve as a true and adequate metaphysical foundation for the universal problems of the modern age and the ages to come. "Philosophers can never hope finally to formulate these metaphysical first principles. Weakness of insight and deficiencies of language stand in the way inexorably."[10] His vital contribution lies in the fact that he once again brought to the forefront the need for attempting to develop an adequate metaphysical system which would bring together all areas of human interest. Whitehead's greatness lies in the open-ended method he developed and presented, affording a foundation for the development of a metaphysical system for each age which will exhibit the true nature of process itself.

II

Some Basic Terms

Our primary consideration is with Whitehead's method, his doctrine of God, and his view of religion. It is impossible to separate these three topics completely from his metaphysical content but, in order that our consideration does not become engulfed by the vastness of the metaphysical system, basic terms will be defined.

Two points should be borne in mind in considering White-head's terms. The first point is that Whitehead considers himself to belong to the philosophical tradition from Plato to the present day. "This nomenclature has been made up to conform to the condition, that, as a theory develops, its technical phraseology should grow out of the usages of the great masters who laid its foundation."[11] His purpose is to use the terms of historical philosophy wherever possible, though at times he fits the meanings to his own particular purpose.

The second point is Whitehead's distrust of language.[12] Language is the tool and at the same time the basic problem of philosophy.[13]

> One source of vagueness is deficiency of language. We can see the variations of meaning; although we cannot verbalize them in any decisive, handy manner. Thus we cannot weave into a train of thought what we can apprehend in flashes. We are left with the deceptive identity of the repeated word.[14]

It is the job of philosophy to use the tool of language but never to allow this tool to become an "absolute" or limiting factor in the search for true expression. The philosopher must constantly re-evaluate his language in order that the symbol "propose the general character of the universe required for that fact."[15] Philosophical language is to be used within the historical tradition of philosophy, but the symbols are to be employed in a relative manner in order that they should not limit the philosophical enterprise.

Whitehead's terms and statements are not always clear and distinct. At times statements are clearer than one would expect. At other times he paints a picture with words in order that the reader may gain a feeling for that which he means to convey. Verbal contradictions seem to abound in Whitehead's writing, if one does not read carefully and make close comparison of texts. William Christian offers an excellent insight into Whitehead's style, which if noted will be of service in understanding Whitehead's terms and the varied manner in which they are used.

> Some of the obscurities can be seen through if one distinguishes three sorts of discourse. In some passages Whitehead is evoking and describing the concrete experiences he takes as his basic data. This we might call presystematic language. In others he is constructing and developing the concepts which compose his categorical scheme. This we might call systematic language. Elsewhere he uses these systematic terms to interpret sense experience, the order of nature, art, morality, or religion. Here he is applying his scheme, and we might call this post-systematic language. These phases of his exposition correspond to the three phases of an airplane flight, with which he compares speculative philosophy. It begins on the ground; it rises into the air; and it returns to earth. Many blunders can be avoided if we do not mistake nonsystematic remarks for systematic ones.16

1.   Actual entity: Actual entities are also termed actual occasions. This represents the final, real thing of which the world or universe is made. An actual entity is a "drop of experience" which in itself constitutes its internal right-to-be. On the basis that actual entities are the only real things, the ontological principle is asserted. On the basis of this principle, all things are positively somewhere in actuality and relatively potential everywhere for the process of another actual entity.

> This ontological principle means that actual entities are the only reasons; so that to search for a reason is to search for one or more actual entities. It follows that any condition to be satisfied by one actual entity in its process expresses a fact either about the "real internal constitutions"

32

of some other actual entities, or about the
"subjective aim" conditioning that process.17

2. Eternal object: If the first type or primary entity is a
temporal actual entity, the second is an eternal object. "Any
entity whose conceptual recognition does not involve a necessary reference to any definite actual entities of the temporal
world is called an 'eternal object.'"18 Eternal objects should
be related to the "Platonic form." The function of an eternal
object is to serve as a potentiality for actual entities. In
other words God supplies to the becoming experience its initial
"subjective aim" in the form of an eternal object. The temporal actual entity is not responsible for formulating its subjective aim, although it is responsible for the way in which this
aim is developed. An eternal object is neutral so far as it relates to its physical ingression in any particular actual entity
of the temporal world. Two points are to be noted. On the
one hand, an eternal object is an individual, which in its own
nontemporal way is what it is. On the other hand, an eternal
object has a "relational essence," which is to say that it cannot
exist except in relation to other eternal objects, actuality generally, and particular temporal actual entities on the basis of
ingression.

3. Process: An actual entity, an experience, can be an-
alyzed into functionings which make up its "process of becoming." These functionings point to the fact that an actual entity includes another entity as an object of its experience.
This act of inclusion is called positive prehension. When an
entity is excluded as an object relating to the process of becoming of that actual entity, this exclusion is called negative
prehension. A prehension of a temporal actual entity is called
a physical prehension. The eternal objects are pure, not actual potentials, and a prehension of an eternal object is called
a conceptual prehension.19

4. Feeling: Feeling is essential to the process of becoming
because on the basis of feeling, prehensions are made and
direction is given to the becoming of the actual occasion. The
complex constitution of a feeling is analyzable into five factors.

> The factors are: (i) the "subject"
> which feels, (ii) the "initial data" which
> are to be felt, (iii) the "elimination" in
> virtue of negative prehensions, (iv) the
> "objective datum" which is felt, (v) the
> "subjective form" which is how that subject
> feels that datum.20

In considering feeling, the lure for feeling must be included. In the subject's act of prehension, the Primordial Nature of God is prehended. The Primordial Nature of God (to be considered under term number seven) serves as a "lure for feeling" in the process of the becoming of an actual entity. In other words, God is responsible for the beginning of the feeling process.

5. Concrescence: This is the process of the coming together into a unity of the different parts of the experience. In the process of feeling, the subject has developed an aim. When the aim of the actual entity occurs in a unity of experience, a concrescence has occurred. The term "satisfaction" refers to the fulfillment of the aim which has occurred in the concrescence. At this stage a new actual entity occurs. When an actual entity occurs there is a new form in the world; it means that novelty has come into the process.

6. Objective Immortality:21 This term refers to the fact that after a temporal entity has reached its satisfaction, it perishes. In the state of perishing, the actual entity enters in the nature of God into a state of objective immortality, in the sense that in this state of "being" it becomes an object of possible prehension for the process of becoming for other actual entities, including God. "It belongs to the nature of a 'being' that it is a potential for every 'becoming.' This is the 'principle of relativity.' "22

7. God: God is an actual entity which is non-temporal. This means that God does not perish and become objectively immortal as temporal actual entities. God's nature can be discussed in three ways. The first is the Primordial Nature of God. In this nature God sustains all eternal objects. In other words, God contains in the eternal objects all the potential "subjective aims" for temporal actual entities. Through this nature God supplies each becoming experience with an eternal object-subjective aim.23 The second is the Consequent Nature of God. "This 'consequent nature' of God is the physical prehension by God of the actualities of the evolving universe."24 In this way God saves the perishing actual entities in his own nature. The third is the Superjective Nature of God. "The 'superjective' nature of God is the character of the pragmatic value of his specific satisfaction qualifying the transcendent creativity in the various temporal instances."25 This is the manner in which God works to bring about good or harmony in the universe instead of evil or destruction. This trinitarian view of God must not be taken to mean that God is three, instead of one concrete actual entity. These three natures of God must be taken into account at all times, or the nature of God is being considered in abstraction.

8. Creativity: Creativity "is that ultimate notion of the highest generality at the base of actuality."26 Creativity is without character or individuality of its own. It is the active, creative force of the universe, being conditioned by the objective immortality of the actual world and by God. By making creativity the ultimate basis of the universe, Whitehead rejects the mechanical view for which the ultimate category is that of cause and effect. Because of creativity, every actual entity, temporal or non-temporal, is to some degree self-creative. Every actual entity, being to some degree self-creative, is a novel being. On the basis of novelty, as stated before, an actual entity is a new form in the universe. The doctrine of creativity points to the fact that constantly new forms are being created and are perishing in the universe.

III

Foundation Principles of Whitehead's Method

In the introduction it was pointed out that Whitehead operates from a historical, scientific, and metaphysical perspective. A review of the interactions of these perspectives will be helpful in understanding Whitehead's metaphysical presuppositions. From the historical perspective, Whitehead tries to show that real progress in history has depended on creative or speculative reason, an open-ended rational process. It is necessary to bear in mind what Whitehead means by the rational process. "Rationalism is the faith or hope that in experience all elements are intrinsically capable of exhibition as examples of general theory."27 Whitehead places his hope and faith in rationalism, but he clearly asserts repeatedly that nothing rests on ultimate authority, that the final court of appeal is to the intrinsic reasonableness of the claims that are being made.28

Within the history of ideas, the areas of philosophy, science and religion have tended mostly to limit this speculative rational process. Philosophy, being conditioned by mathematics, has centered on logical problems, basing its premises on the obvious in life.29 By placing its emphasis on the more obvious in life, it has failed in its purpose to explain the emergence of the more abstract from the more concrete.30 In this development of thought, philosophy has separated itself and has been separated from scientific inquiry; thus, the great limitation of modern philosophy is that its endeavours have not thrown light on scientific principles. "A philosophical system should present an elucidation of concrete fact from which the sciences abstract. Also the sciences should find their principles in the concrete facts which a philosophic system presents."31 Philosophy cannot perform its full function so long as it remains separate from the thoughts and findings of any discipline. The great task of modern philosophy is to relate the one and the many.32 To accomplish this task, philosophy must perform its proper role of harmonizing the various abstractions of methodological thought.33

Science has come to limit itself to the positivistic school of thought, refusing to risk its findings to the method of speculation.34 In this way, science has cut itself off from the other disciplines and has, therefore, not performed its proper function of supplying these other disciplines with information which would transcend the immediate scientific concern.

> Science has never shaken off the impress of its origin in the historical revolt of the later Renaissance. It has remained predominantly an antirationalistic movement, based upon a naive faith. . . .Science repudiates philosophy. In other words, it has never cared to justify its faith or to explain its meanings.35

In another statement Whitehead makes explicit the general inherent danger in modern science.

> Its methodological procedure is exclusive and intolerant, and rightly so. It fixes attention on a definite group of abstractions, neglects everything else, and elicits every scrap of information and theory which is relevant to what it has retained.36

Religion has served as another limiting factor to the speculative process. The limitations of religion will be considered in a later section. It will suffice for the present to say that in general religion has limited itself to tradition, cutting itself off from all disciplines which might effectively question the validity of the traditional "truths" and resting its case against speculation and other insights on "absolute" dogmas.37

To put the matter in another way, these three spheres have tried in their different ways to separate the mind from the body, and vice versa.38 Emotion and reason have not been seen properly as a part of the same total process of human understanding. Man has been presented with a fragmented internal and external universe; on the one hand, the mind is separated ultimately from the body, and on the other, reason is separated from emotion. This situation has been made worse by the assertion, on the part of philosophy and theology, of secret insight into a God outside the universe who is responsible for the fragmented condition but unconditioned by the fragmented situation. With each discipline working with its own method separately, the speculative process has been limited; and, thus, the progressive development of civilization has been limited. The need of the day is for a return to a true speculation which will combine all the disciplines by offering a method which will draw together all methods while at the same time transcending the procedure and limiting effect of method itself. History has shown that the progress of civilization occurs because of the process of creative speculation. This happens because men are willing to risk themselves and the old order with its limited method. Creative speculation is the process which joins the body and the mind, in order that man can experience and begin to understand true "feeling."39 Whitehead intends his philosophy to serve this process of experience and understanding. At the same time he cautions, lest his philosophy or method be used as a dogma which holds back the true process.

From his trinitarian perspective, Whitehead asserts that all judgments are made from some general systematic metaphysical scheme.40 By this he means that all thought operates from some metaphysical position, no matter how inadequate be the position.

Whitehead's own philosophical method and position presupposes a metaphysical scheme. Aspects to the presuppositions of this scheme will be presented. Although he is basically concerned with the individual, his view of the universe offers a good starting-point in understanding his metaphysical presupposition.

There is no reason to hold that confusion is less fundamental than is order. Our task is to evolve a general concept which allows room for both; and which also suggests the path for the enlargement of our penetration. My suggestion is that we start from the notion of two aspects of the Universe. It includes a factor of unity, involving in its essence the connexity of things, unity of purpose, and unity of enjoyment. The whole notion of importance is referent to this ultimate unity. There is also equally fundamental in the Universe, a factor of multiplicity. There are many actualities, each with its own experience, enjoying individually, and yet requiring other.

Any description of the unity will require the many actualities; and any description of the many will require the notion of the unity from which importance and purpose is derived. By reason of the essential individuality of the many things, there are conflicts of finite realizations. Thus the summation of the many into the one, and the derivation of importance from the one into many, involves the notion of disorder, of conflict, of frustration.

These are the primary aspects of the universe which common sense brooding over the aspects of existence hands over to philosophy for elucidation into some coherence of understanding.41

Man is part of this universe, and in no way can he experience except as part of the universe. "The doctrine that I maintain is that neither physical nature nor life can be understood unless we fuse them together as essential factors in the composition of 'really real' things whose inter-connections and individual characters constitute the universe."42 Everything that man knows about himself in the universe is through experience. This experience is to be understood as a total body-experience--a combination of extensive body-reason and extensive body-emotion.43 The total body never experiences itself in isolation but always in relation to the universe. Thus all experience has two sides: (1) the individual self, and (2) its signification in the universe.44 Man is able to understand himself in relation to the universe by the process of creative imagination, using Whitehead's method which will be discussed later. Without this process, he is able only to formulate dogmatic propositions from a limited perspective. This process also rests on the pre-supposition that there are universal principles, eternal objects, by which man's experience is conditioned.45 Whitehead assumes that all experience is connected and inter-related, so that the basic premises of one experience can be used to help understand the pattern of other experience. All experience can be connected and understood on the basis of general principles.

Whitehead states these general principles as metaphysical assumptions. "Presentational immediacy" is defined as "the 'mode' in which the contemporary world is consciously prehended as a continuum of extensive relations."46 On the basis of presentational immediacy, two metaphysical assumptions are asserted. (1) The first is "that the actual world, in so far as it is a community of entities which are settled, actual, and already become, conditions and limits the potentiality for creativeness beyond itself."47 (2) "The second metaphysical assumption is that the real potentialities relative to all standpoints are coordinated as diverse determinations of one extensive continuum."48 From the assumption that no static maintenance of perfection is possible, Whitehead asserts three metaphysical principles. "One principle is that the very essence of real actuality--that is, of the complete real--is process. Thus each actual thing is only to be understood in terms of its be-

coming and perishing."49   The second metaphysical principle
"is the doctrine that any occasion of actuality is in its own
nature finite.   There is no totality which is the harmony of all
perfections.   Whatever is realized in any one occasion of experience necessarily excludes the unbounded welter of contrary
possibilities.   There are always "others," which might have
been and are not."50   The third principle is that:

>The individual, real facts of the past
>lie at the base of our immediate experience
>in the present. They are the reality from
>which the occasion springs, the reality
>from which it derives its source of emo-
>tion, from which it inherits its purpose, to
>which it directs its passions. At the base
>of experience there is a welter of feeling,
>derived from individual realities or directed
>towards them. Thus for strength of ex-
>perience we require to discriminate the
>component factors, each as an individual
>"It" with its own significance.51

As Whitehead develops his system of categories, other
metaphysical principles are presented, but the later principles
are basically derived from these fundamental principles. The
basic ones presented should serve our purpose for considering
his method.

IV

Structure of Whitehead's Method

Whitehead's method is a method of speculative reason for speculative philosophy. His method is an attempt to transcend the limiting methods of particular disciplines. Previously, philosophy has been divided into schools of rationalism, empiricism and idealism--even if there has seldom been an absolute division. Whitehead rejects the position of idealism because it has not taken seriously the scientific developments and insights of the modern period.52 It is asserted that both rationalism and empiricism have contributed isolated insights, but they have been limited by the narrowness of their basic presuppositions and methods. Whitehead's method is to combine rationalism and empiricism, and by this combination to do away with the limiting factors of each position. Emphasis is not given to philosophy but to speculative philosophy. The task of "speculative philosophy is the endeavour to frame a coherent, logical, and necessary system of general ideas in terms of which every element of our experience can be interpreted."53 By using the terms "coherent" and "logical," he points to the rational side of the method. This rational side permits the possibility of an understanding of experience. There is also an empirical side of the method, which can be expressed by the terms "applicable" and "adequate." The empirical side of the method asserts that all rational postulates must be tested in experience according to their applicability or adequacy.

Whitehead has developed his method out of the felt need that modern man, especially in the sciences and religion, needs a more adequate foundation for gaining an insight into the nature of the universe. He asserts that "the main evidence that a methodology is worn out comes when progress within it no longer deals with main issues."54 It was evident to Whitehead that the method of modern science had begun to wear out. It has been the purpose of the method of science to fix attention on a definite group of abstractions, neglecting everything else, and eliciting every scrap of information and theory relevant to what is retained. Within limits, this method is valid and has proved successful. On the basis of this method, however, a dangerous fallacy has occurred which "is to make observations upon one scale of magnitude and to translate their results into laws valid for another scale."55 Another limitation of science, from the perspective of particular scientific fields,

43

has been its indifference to great areas of data and the possibility of larger amounts of future data. So long as the relevance of evidence is dictated by theory, it is not possible to prove or disprove a theory by evidence which the theory dismisses as irrelevant. Science in its limiting functions has shown the need for a more open-ended method which will keep the theory from functioning as a restrictive factor in the evaluation of what is relevant data.56   "The science of the future depends for its ready progress upon the antecedent elucidation of hypothetical complexities of connection, as yet unobserved in nature."57   Reference will be made later to the limitation of religion and its method. Whitehead evaluates the contribution of science and religion, realizing them both to be vital, and asserts the need for a method that will offer more adequate service to mankind. Our understanding has revealed an extremely complex state of existence, and it is necessary for man to have adequate tools for considering every possibility in order that he may live more fully.

> We need to entertain every prospect
> of novelty, every chance that could result
> in new combinations. But at the same time
> we need to entertain those with skeptical
> examination, and subject them to the most
> impartial scrutiny, for the probability is
> that nine hundred and ninety-nine of them
> will come to nothing, either because worth-
> less in themselves or because we shall not
> know how to elicit their values; but we had
> better entertain them all, however skepti-
> cally, for the thousandth idea may be the
> one that will change the world.58

The spirit of the speculative method is that of curiosity going on an adventure.59   Curiosity is the craving of reason that the facts discriminated in experience be understood.

> It means the refusal to be satisfied
> with the bare welter of fact, or even with
> the bare habit of routine. The first step
> in science and philosophy has been made
> when it is grasped that every routine ex-
> emplifies a principle which is capable of
> statement in abstraction from its particular
> exemplifications. The curiosity, which is
> the gadfly driving civilization from its an-
> cient safeties, is the desire to state the
> principles in their abstraction. In this
> curiosity there is a ruthless element which
> in the end disturbs.60

44

Even though Whitehead gives great attention to the need for speculative thought, he is careful to balance the hope offered in his method by his evaluation of the possibility of proof.

> Unless proof has produced self-evidence and thereby rendered itself unnecessary, it has issued in a second-rate state of mind, producing action devoid of understanding. Self-evidence is the basic fact on which all greatness supports itself. But "proof" is one of the routes by which self-evidence is often obtained. . . .It follows that philosophy, in any proper sense of the term, cannot be proved. For proof is based upon abstraction. Philosophy is either self-evident, or it is not philosophy . . . .The aim of philosophy is sheer disclosure.61

Speculative philosophy cannot be proved in the normally accepted sense because its task is disclosure. This does not relieve speculative generalizations from the responsibility of being tested by the empirical and rational means, previously mentioned. At the same time man does himself a great injustice if he dismisses the speculative process because it does not conform to the purely empirical school. The history of civilization has shown that fear of error is the death of progress, and that an open-ended search for truth is the backbone of progress.62 If progress is man's goal, history has clearly shown that the only hope for attaining this goal lies in speculative process. "Abstract speculation has been the salvation of the world--speculation which made systems and then transcended them, speculations which ventured to the furthest limit of abstraction. To set limits to speculation is treason to the future."63

Whitehead's method is different in important respects from other philosophical methods. Thus Whitehead's method differs from the procedure of rationalism. Historically, one major view has been that the task of philosophy is to indicate premises which are certain, clear, and distinct, and then on the basis of these premises to develop a deductive system of thought.64 This represents the more logical school of philosophy which follows the pattern of mathematics. The influence of mathematics was positive in that it provided reason with a more adequate means of testing, freeing the reasoning process "from its sole dependence on mystic vision and fanciful suggestion."65 It is assumed by this school that the premises can be discerned easily, and the major responsibility rests in the deductive process. Whitehead asserts that man cannot know easily, clear and distinct premises which are of ultimate concern. The premises that are obvious are of little value, and indeed generally obscure for man what are the really important premises. That job of philosophy is then shifted from the deductive concern to the search for the premises that are not obvious but are of essential importance.

The empirical character of Whitehead's position is often misunderstood by identifying it with the more traditional forms of dogmatic empiricism. This misunderstanding can be corrected by taking seriously Whitehead's assertion:

> The unempirical character of the philosophical school derived from Hume cannot be too often insisted upon. The true empirical doctrine is that physical feelings are in their origin vectors, and that the genetic process of concrescence introduces the elements which emphasize privacy.66

Whitehead points out that "the philosophy of organism is apt to emphasize just those elements in the writings of the masters which subsequent systematizers have put aside."67   This he does, in developing the empirical character of his position in relation to Locke and Hume. Space will not permit a full consideration of Whitehead's evaluation of the relation of process philosophy to traditional empiricism, but we will try to indicate the general trend of his thought.68

Whitehead points out that John Locke, in his later writings, most fully anticipated the main position of process philosophy.69   Locke's nearest approach to the process position occurred when he said that the mind is furnished with a great number of simple ideas via the senses. The simple ideas often go together and form more complex ideas. Exterior things are responsible for the fact that minds entertain these ideas. Locke did not develop this view adequately, but it laid the foundation for bridging the separation between mind and eternal reality. Whitehead developed this line of reasoning in terms of "the vector character of primary feelings."70   Locke also insisted that the notion of "substance" involved the notion of "power." Process philosophy develops this insight and "holds that in order to understand 'power,' we must have a correct notion of how each individual actual entity contributes to the datum from which its successors arise and to which they must conform."71 His view of "power" made possible "change," but "Locke misses one essential doctrine, namely, that the doctrine of internal relations makes it possible to attribute 'change' to any actual entity."72   Whitehead's basic difference from

46

Locke is indicated by his criticism that Locke inherited, from Descartes, the view of "dualism whereby minds are one kind of particulars, and natural entities are another kind of particulars, and also the subject-predicate dogma."73   Thus, his philosophy is limited by the unconscious and uncriticized assumption "that logical simplicity can be identified with priority in the process constituting an experient occasion."74   For Whitehead, the more conservative side of Locke's anti-metaphysical position is an inadequate empirical approach, but some of his less developed thoughts point the way towards a more adequate empiricism.

> Locke enunciates the main doctrines of the philosophy of organism, namely: the principle of relativity, the relational character of eternal objects, whereby they constitute the forms of the objectifications of actual entities for each other; the composite character of an actual entity (i.e., a substance); the notion of "power" as making a principal ingredient in that of actual entity (substance). In this latter notion, Locke adumbrates both the ontological principle, and also the principle that the "power" of one actual entity on the other is simply how the former is objectified in the constitution of the other.75

Whitehead believes the more skeptical, dogmatic empiricism of Hume to be a violation of empiricism, because it is based on the more conservative side of Locke's thoughts. Hume's skeptical reduction of knowledge is based on the tacit presupposition of the subject-mind with its contents as predicates.76 Locke's use of the term "idea," making room for complex ideas, is rejected and replaced by Hume with the more limited notion of a simple idea derived from simple impressions. In this way he re-asserts the "fallacy of simple location." Yet, as Hume develops his position, the doctrine of "repetition" becomes essential.

> The notion of "simple location" is inconsistent with any admission of "repetition;" Hume's difficulties arise from the fact that he starts with simple locations and ends with repetition. In the organic philosophy the notion of repetition is fundamental. The doctrine of objectification is an endeavor to express how what is settled in actuality is repeated under limitations, so as to be "given" for immediacy. Later,

47

in discussing "time," this doctrine will be
termed the doctrine of "objective" immortal-
ity.77

The attempt to combine these two doctrines is doomed to
failure, and it is this which gives rise to all Hume's prob-
lems.78   In trying to deal with this combination, he places
"cause and effect" beyond the immediate impression of our
memory and our sense. Operating within this conflict of doctrine, Hume also does not deal with the problem of "novel com-
pound idea" and "imaginative freedom."79   His inconsistency
becomes compounded because he is not able entirely to disre-
gard common sense.80 Whitehead devotes much time to Hume's
common sense assertion that the eye sees, implying that what
Hume really means by "see" is "feel." Whitehead is trying to
get away from the abstract mechanical associations of "impression" in order to point out that in normal unsophisticated
experience every perception has a "feeling-tone."

> The crude aboriginal character of di-
> rect perception is inheritance. What is in-
> herited is feeling-tone with evidence of its
> origin: in other words, vector feeling-tone
> differentiates itself into various types of
> sense--those of touch, sight, smell, etc,--
> each transmuted into a definite prehension
> of tonal contemporary nexus by the final
> percipient.81

Hume does not adequately take into account the complex nature
of sense experience and, therefore, presents a false empirical
position. For Whitehead, an adequate empirical approach must
be based on his dictum: "How an actual entity becomes constitutes what that actual entity is."82

Even though Hume's empiricism is limited by the doctrine
of "simple location," his philosophy does make a marked contribution to the philosophy of organism. His most important contribution is proclaiming "the bankruptcy of morphology."

> Hume's train of thought unwittingly
> emphasizes "process." His very skepticism
> is nothing but the discovery that there is
> something in the world which cannot be
> expressed in analytic propositions. Hume
> discovered that "We murder to dissect."
> He did not say this, because he belonged
> to the mid-eighteenth century: and so left
> the remark to Wordsworth. But, in effect,
> Hume discovered that an actual entity is at

once a process, and is atomic; so that in no sense is it the sum of its parts. Hume proclaimed the bankruptcy of morphology.83

Hume's account of process is described as occurring within "the soul." In process philosophy, Hume's "soul" and Hume's and Locke's "mind" are designated either as "the actual entity" or as "the actual occasion."84   The philosophy of organism also uses Hume's doctrine of "feeling," extending it into the doctrine of "subjective form."85   Whitehead does not assert that he has solved the difficulty which puzzled Hume, but he does believe that his metaphysical position offers the possibility of complete solution.

> Hume's philosophy found nothing in any single instance to justify the mind's expectation. Accordingly he was reduced to explaining the origin of the mind's expectation otherwise than by its rational justification. It follows, that if we are to get out of Hume's difficulty, we must find something in each single instance, which would justify the belief. The key to the mystery is not to be found in the accumulation of instances, but in the intrinsic character of each instance. When we have found that, we will have struck at the heart of Hume's argument.86

The empirical character of Whitehead's position is actually an alteration of the traditional empiricism associated with Locke and Hume.87   Whitehead's empiricism is based on the experience of the total organism in relation to the event. This is an inversion of the emphasis by Hume upon a simple idea derived from a simple impression. Hume pointed out the complex character of perception, according to the doctrine of secondary quality. This was tacitly presupposed by Locke in his discussion of color as a secondary quality. Considering the complex character of perception, Whitehead draws the conclusion that the character of sense perception is superficial.

> . . .sense-perception for all its practical importance is very superficial in its disclosure of the nature of things. . . .My quarrel with modern Epistemology concerns its exclusive stress upon sense-perception for the provision of data respecting Nature. Sense-perception does not   provide

the data in terms of which we interpret
it.88

For Whitehead, theory dictates method, and his basic affirmation is of process which asserts the interrelatedness of
experience and the development from simple events to more
complex events. He alters Locke's and Hume's doctrine of sen-
sationalism by placing the emphasis upon the whole organism
related to the experience instead of the five senses.89   By
giving emphasis to the relatedness of the whole organism,
Whitehead attempts to take into account the depth feeling tones
of the experience and the intuitions which are given in the
total experience. In taking such a stance, Whitehead is alter-
ing Hume's introspective analysis by a primary aesthetic emphasis within the context of his process theory. This theory
attempts to take into account the cosmological and environmental factors which condition the experience.90   For Whitehead
there is a depth, indeed an infinitude of actuality, which is
not revealed by the superficial level of sense perception.

> In other words, reaction to the envi-
> ronment is not in proportion to clarity of
> sensory experience. Any such doctrine
> would sweep away the whole of modern
> physical science as being expressed in
> terms of irrelevancies. Reaction does not
> depend upon sense-experience for its ini-
> tiation.

> Now confine the argument to human
> experience, which we know at first hand.
> This experience does not depend for its
> excellence simply upon clarity of sense-
> experience. The specialist in clarity,
> sinks to an animal level--the hound for
> smell, the eagle for sight.

> Human beings are amateurs in sense-
> experience. The direct, vivid clarity does
> not dominate so as to obscure the infinite
> variety involved in the composition of real-
> ity. The sense-experience is an abstrac-
> tion which illustrates and stimulates the
> completeness of actuality. It increases im-
> portance. But the importance thus elicited
> is more than a color-scheme of red, white,
> and blue. It involves the infinitude of
> actuality, hidden in its finitude of realiza-
> tion.91

Whitehead asserts the necessity for man to go on a speculative adventure in order to understand the depth of experience. By placing his emphasis upon cosmology and speculative
philosophy, within the context of his process theory, Whitehead
asserts an empirical emphasis which attempts to go beyond the
superficial level of sense-experience expressed in dogmatic empiricism. Whitehead repudiates many habits of philosophical
thought, including dogmatic empiricism. These may be listed
as:

(i)   The distrust of speculative philoso-
        phy.
(ii)   The trust in language as an adequate
        expression of propositions.
(iii)   The mode of philosophical thought
        which implies, and is implied by, the
        faculty-psychology.
(iv)   The subject-predicate form of expres-
        sion.
(v)   The sensationalist doctrine of percep-
        tion.
(vi)   The doctrine of vacuous actuality.
(vii)   The Kantian doctrine of the objective
        world as a theoretical construct from
        purely subjective experience.
(viii) Arbitrary deductions in ex absurdo
        arguments.
(ix)   Belief that logical inconsistencies can
        indicate anything else than some
        antecedent errors.92

Whitehead designates his method for this task of speculative philosophy to be the method of "imaginative rationalization,"93 or in other words the method of "descriptive generalization."94 This method might well be called the method of
empirical analysis and speculative generalization. Based on an
analysis of experience, philosophical generalizations are postulated through the use of creative imagination. Then through
an empirical process these generalizations are tested in experience to see if they are applicable and adequate.

In line with his metaphysical presuppositions, Whitehead's
method begins with man in the actual world. Man in experience is considered from different perspectives. One perspective is that which views man in general as he tries to develop
the "art of life." "The art of life is first to be alive, secondly
to be alive in a satisfactory way, and thirdly to acquire an increase in satisfaction."95 The history of civilization has shown
that man has struggled with these three stages of development
in order fully to develop his life. As man has struggled to

acquire an increase in his satisfaction he has been guided by a
desire and purpose for this increase. Any method that omits
or does not allow for this purpose serves as a limiting factor in
man's development.

An infusion of novelty occurs in each stage in the progressive art of life, making possible the fulfillment of that
stage. In other words, each stage in developing that art of
life needs its own method. As one stage is fulfilled, it is
necessary that a new and more adequate method develop as the
foundation and directional force for the next stage. This new
method is made possible as the old method includes and is
transformed by the infusion of novelty into the situation.96
Reason is essential to this development of the art of life. Man
is able to move from one state to another because of the functioning of his reason: "the primary function of Reason is the
direction of the attack on the environment."97

> The essence of Reason in its lowliest
> forms is its judgement upon flashes of
> novelty which is relevant to appetition but
> not yet to action. In the stabilized life
> there is no room for Reason. The method-
> ology has sunk from a method of novelty
> into a method of repetition. Reason is the
> organ of emphasis upon novelty. It pro-
> vides the judgement by which realization in
> idea obtains the emphasis by which it
> passes into realization in purpose, and
> thence its realization in fact.98

There is contrast within the scope of method as it develops,
and the good life is attained by the enjoyment of the contrast.
Within this development, man's appetition is working within a
framework of order, which makes it possible for reason working
within this order to provide a direction of "the upward trend."
Thus, reason and purpose cannot be separated. When reason
operates within a method that includes novelty and purpose, an
upward direction is given in the struggle for the art of life.
The force working reason is "fatigue." "Fatigue is the antith-
esis of Reason. . . .Fatigue means the operation of excluding
the impulse towards novelty."99 The goal of the method is to
exclude the force of fatigue by basing the method on Reason
functioning within a situation which includes novelty, making
possible an upward purpose for man in the art of life.

At another time, Whitehead's method begins with man
viewing the world through his immediate experience and trying
to understand what it means. By thought, he attempts to
make clear his immediate experience, "The starting point for

thought is the analytic observation of components of the experience."100   At this point, and at all points, the use of language is of essential importance.   Words must be used and tested to be sure that they represent the most adequate mode of expressing what is meant to be conveyed.   One can never observe or express the total actual world.   The mistake comes as the attempt is made to pin down what the world means to the experience we have.   Whitehead asserts that this is the fallacy of the Baconian method of induction.   What is needed in trying to understand experience is imagination and analysis and not a resting on obvious but unimportant premises.   What is essential is to develop adequate general premises in order to understand the experience and its relation to other experiences.   In order that we may see the relationship of one experience to other experiences, an analysis of the experience into its different parts is necessary.   It is important that this analysis be done in a systematic fashion, using language expressive of the situation.   On the basis of analysis and the free play of imagination, controlled by the requirements of coherence and logic, philosophical generalizations are formulated from the observed experience.   After generalizations are developed concerning the experience, they must be tested empirically, to see if they comply with the actual world.   The value of the philosophical generalization is limited, if it does not comply with the actual world of the particular experience and other experiences.   At the same time the generalization is limited if it is not interesting; "it is more important that a proposition be interesting than that it be true."101   If a generalization is to provide the maximum benefit, it must apply to reality, while at the same time it must be interesting.   Whitehead describes this process in the following manner:

> The true method of discovery is like the flight of an airplane.   It starts from the ground of particular observation; it makes a flight into the air of imaginative generalization; and it again lands for renewed observation rendered acute by rational interpretation.   The reason for the success of this method of imaginative rationalization is that, when the method of difference fails, factors which are constantly present may yet be observed under the influence of imaginative thought.   Such thought supplies the differences which the direct observation lacks.102

In order that imaginative construction may perform its function, it must adhere to disciplined conditions.   "This construction must have its origin in the generalization of particu-

lar factors discerned in particular topics of human interest."103
A philosophical generalization is set forth on the basis of general observation from the perspective of some particular topic
of human interest.

> Philosophic thought has to start from
> some limited section of our experience --
> from epistemology, or from natural science,
> or from theology, or from mathematics.
> Also the investigation always retains the
> taint of its starting point. Every starting
> point has its merits, and its selection must
> depend upon the individual philosopher.104

This topic of human interest, whether it be theology, physics,
or history, affords the observer a theory or "working hypothesis" from which to consider the experience.105   Without a
"working hypothesis" the observation is not directed, and the
observer cannot know what to look for in the experience.
Whitehead strongly insists upon this doctrine: "Such an hypothesis directs observation, and decides on the mutual relevance
of various types of evidence. In short, it prescribes method.
To venture upon productive thought without such an explicit
theory is to abandon one-self to the doctrines derived from
one's grandfather."106

It is not enough to show that a philosophical generalization is adequate in its particular area of human interest. "The
success of the imaginative experiment is always to be tested by
the applicability of its results beyond the restricted locus from
which it originated."107 It is necessary to test a philosophical
generalization which is based on one area of human interest in
other areas of human interest. By this method of cross-testing, a generalization should show, if it is adequate, that all
experiences are connected and interrelated. In this way the
basic premises of one experience can be used to help understand the patterns of other experiences. This aspect of the
method supports Whitehead's presupposition that all experiences
can be connected and understood on the basis of general premises. It also protects his method from a fallacy attributed to
other methods; "since all things are connected, any system
which omits some things must necessarily suffer from such limitation."108   It is Whitehead's purpose to have his method begin with a particular area of interest, but not to be limited by
the traditional method of that area. He overcomes this potential limitation by requiring that generalizations be made on the
basis of the available evidence from the perspective of one
particular area and then that these generalizations be tested
from the perspective of other areas of interest. In this way,
all areas of human interest and insights are called upon to

participate in the development of principles which will transcend their own area of concern.

For imaginative construction to be adequate, it must also seek two rationalistic ideals: coherence and logical perfection. Without coherence, there is the arbitrary disconnection of basic principles. "The coherence, which the system seeks to preserve, is the discovery that the process, or concrescence, of any actual entity involves the other actual entities among its components. In this way, the obvious solidarity of the world receives its explanation."109 It is very difficult to develop the scheme into a logical truth. Logical perfection should be the goal; at the same time the logical propositions must always be under review and never used as absolute logical statements. "The scheme should therefore be stated with the utmost precision and definiteness, to allow for such argumentation."110 A philosophical generalization without these ideals may not be true to the observed experience and, thus, may not be related logically to other areas of human interest. Whitehead asserts that the lack of these ideals gives rise to the chief error in philosophy, which is overstatement. There are two forms of overstatement. The first is called "the fallacy of misplaced concreteness."

> One form is what I have termed elsewhere, the "fallacy of misplaced concreteness." This fallacy consists in neglecting the degree of abstraction involved when an actual entity is considered merely so far as it exemplifies certain categories of thought. There are aspects of actualities which are simply ignored so long as we restrict thought to these categories. Thus the success of a philosophy is to be measured by its comparative avoidance of this fallacy, when thought is restricted within its categories.111

Here the generalization does not take into account all aspects of the observed experience, and thus forms its observations on the basis of restricted insight. The generalization is not coherent with what is actually given. "The other form of overstatement consists in a false estimate of logical procedure in respect to certainty, and in respect to premises."112 The generalization cannot claim tentative certainty until it has been logically tested in a variety of areas of human interest. Without these ideals, adequate philosophical generalizations are developed on the basis of chance. Generalizations based on chance are often presented as dogmatic statements of what is obvious. Such generalizations do not take into consideration the complexity of reality and are inadequate. Adequate philosophical generalizations can only be tentative formulations of ultimate generalities. The purpose of Whitehead's method is to afford a transcendence of what is obvious in order that adequate philosophical generalizations can be established. The philosophical generalizations are never final, but always open to new tests based on new observation and generalization. Although no rationalistic scheme offers absolute certainty, it should be kept in mind that "the verification of a rationalistic scheme is to be sought in its general success, and not in the peculiar certainty, or initial clarity, of its first principles."113 On the basis of the novelty of experience and observation, philosophical generalizations offer new insight into the structure of life. Whitehead offers a summary statement which describes the way in which his method of speculative reason brings together the empirical and rational interests without their limitations in order to gain this new insight into the structure of life.

> The speculative Reason works in two ways so as to submit itself to the authority of facts without loss of its mission to transcend the existing analysis of facts. In one way it accepts the limitations of a special topic, such as a science or a practical methodology. It then seeks speculatively to enlarge and recast the categorical ideas within the limits of that topic. This is speculative Reason in its closest alliance with the methodological Reason.

> In the other way, it seeks to build a cosmology expressing the general nature of the world as disclosed in human interest. It has already been pointed out, that in order to keep such a cosmology in contact with reality, account must be taken of the welter of established institutions constituting the structures of human society throughout the ages. It is only in this way that we can appeal to the widespread effective elements in the experience of mankind. What these institutions stood for in the experience of their contemporaries, represents the massive facts of ultimate authority.114

The final test of a philosophical position is not finality but progress. Generalizations cannot be limited to specific areas of human interest, and thus become dogmas which are important but limited truth. If generalizations are proved to be final, they are inadequate because they do not afford insight into the progressive character of the universe. What is needed is the development of a scheme of ideas that can serve as the most general interpretative system for experience. It is only by developing ideas into a system that the true adjustment of ideas can be explored, that they can be properly investigated and tested in order to establish their tenability as metaphysical ultimates. Whitehead asserts this view when he says that "philosophy will not regain its proper status until the gradual elaboration of categorical schemes, definitely stated at each stage of progress, is recognized as its proper objective."115

Whitehead's method serves as the tool in his attempt to elaborate a metaphysical scheme, which is as detailed as possible, and in light of his scheme, to investigate the major philosophical problems. This scheme is always subject to the tests of coherence, consistency, universality, applicability, and adequacy. Yet, Whitehead's method for speculative Reason is different from other methods in that it is a method which is supposed to make possible the transcendence of the limitations of method itself.116 On the one hand, this means that this method makes possible the development of a new method. "The speculative Reason produces that accumulation of theoretical understanding which at critical moments enables a transition to be made toward new methodologies. Also the discoveries of the practical understanding provide the raw material necessary for the success of speculative Reason."117 On the other hand, this method does more than provide for the possibility of the development of a new method. "Reason which is methodic is content to limit itself within the bounds of a successful method . . . .Reason which is speculative questions the methods, refusing to let them rest."118 This method is open-ended. It questions the very basis of the validity of method itself. The essential spirit of Whitehead's method is that no factors within the method, or the method itself as a whole, be allowed to limit the search of understanding in the light of experience. The method must be broad enough to include all evidence and all data. It should include all the sciences, whether the science be physics or theology. At the same time the method must serve to restrain the aberrations of mere undisciplined imagination.

> The basis of all authority is the supremacy of fact over thought. Yet this contrast of fact and thought can be conceived fallaciously. For thought is a factor in the fact of experience. Thus the immediate fact is what it is, partly by reason of the thought involved in it. . . .The

supremacy of fact over thought means that
even the utmost flight of speculative
thought should have its measure of truth
. . . .The proper satisfaction to be derived from speculative thought is elucidation. It is for this reason that fact is supreme over thought. This supremacy is
the basis of authority. . . .In this way
there is the progress from thought to
practice, and regress from practice to the
same thought. This interplay of thought
and practice is the supreme authority. It
is the test by which the charlatanism of
speculation is restrained.119

V

The Metaphysical Scheme from

the Perspective of Method

In making a complete study of Whitehead, the next step would be to present an exposition of Whitehead's metaphysical scheme. Such an exposition is beyond the limitations of this chapter, although an evaluation of part of the metaphysical scheme from the perspective of method will be helpful. To accomplish this task, a brief sketch of the metaphysical scheme concerning the evaluation of an actual entity will be presented. On the basis of this sketch, an evaluation will be made from the perspective of method. It is necessary to bear in mind that Whitehead has indicated three major philosophical problems which his method is supposed to help solve. On the one hand, the method is to help deal with the philosophical problem of the one and many. On the other hand, the method is to deal with the issue of efficient and final causes. Both of these problems are a part of the third, which is the problem of permanence and change. It will be necessary to evaluate how far Whitehead's method, as related to the metaphysical scheme of an actual entity, helps to solve these philosophical problems.

Whitehead begins with man in the universe and states that the only basis on which man can make judgments and evaluations is his experience. It has already been stated that a "drop of experience" is an actual entity. Man has experiences, or in some way stands in relation to the process of becoming an actual entity. At the same time man is not himself an actual entity. Rather, man is a collection of prehensions transmitted from one actual occasion to another. "The defining characteristic of a living person is some definite type hybrid prehensions transmitted from one occasion to another."120 This definition assumes that there is a definite, efficient causal relationship between an actual entity in the past or present and actual entities which will come into being in the future. Man realizes that a certain actual entity has occurred within his frame of reference. Upon consideration of the experience, there appear to be obvious causes. Certain sense-data were present to which my senses responded. These senses are a part of the body and seem to have played a definite role in the experience. "We feel with the body. There may be some further specialization into a particular organ of sensation; but in any case the 'witness' of the body is an ever-present, though elusive, element in our preceptions of presentational immediacy."121 Yet it is difficult to know where the body ends and external influences begin. Upon second thought, the definite contributions of the senses do not seem as obvious, and so it becomes necessary to make a more detailed analysis of the actual entity.

Since by definition actual entities are the only real things of which the universe is made, the analysis must confine itself to the particular actual entity, and other actual entities which may have influenced it. In other words, this analysis operates on the ontological principle which states that the reason for things is to be found always in the composite nature of definite actual entities.122   Whitehead concludes: "I hold that these unities of existence, these occasions of experience, are the real things which in their collective unity compose the evolving universe, ever plunging into the creative advance."123   The notions of "creative advance" must be considered. On the basis of reflection, one realizes that there was a time when each experience had not occurred. Each actual entity has come into being through some process. Since this "coming into being" affects every actual entity, not just the one under consideration, it is necessary to assume that there is some force in operation which serves as the fundamental thrust within the process of becoming in all occasions. On the basis of the history of philosophy, it has been asserted that this force is "God," generally a supernatural God operating outside the universe and responsible for the creation of the universe. It is obvious that the actual entities which occur bring both harmony and destruction to the universe, or in more theological terms, some are good and some are evil. This force cannot be God, since to make God responsible for good and evil would indicate a contradiction within the nature of God. In the light of the data from the natural sciences, it is difficult to conceive of a force outside the universe, because this would make the universe finite. It is true that we do not talk of an infinite universe today in any absolute sense, but rather, contend that on the basis of the information available it seems more logical to work from the general theory of an infinite universe. From the perspective of the issue of good and evil and the general theory of an infinite universe, this basic force is considered the primary force of the universe itself. Whitehead uses the term "creativity" to indicate this force: "it is that ultimate notion of the highest generality at the base of actuality."124   In our analysis of an actual entity, it is possible to assume that any actual entity receives its basic thrust in the process of becoming from the basic force of the universe, the principle of creativity.

60

In an analysis of an actual entity, the next step will be to consider the other temporal actual entities which have contributed to the process of a new actual entity occurring. These other actual entities have served as objects for the becoming experience. This function by which the becoming actual entity considers other actual entities as objects is called "prehension." The becoming experience is presented with an infinite number of actual entities as objects. Since all these actual entities cannot work in harmony to help formulate the becoming actual occasion, it is necessary that the occasion be selective. Thus, Whitehead develops the terms "positive prehension" and "negative prehension." A positive prehension, on this physical-temporal level, is the act by which the becoming experience includes other actual entities in its becoming process. When an object is excluded from contributing positively to the process of becoming, this act is designated a negative prehension. "It is the mark of a high-grade organism to eliminate, by negative prehension, the irrelevant accidents in its environment, and to elicit massive attention to every variety of systematic order." 125 By assuming that some are included and some rejected, we are asserting that this becoming experience had the possibility of being other than it came to be. Because of our human limitations and the limitations of our technical tools, it is impossible to make an analysis which will explain the infinite number of actual entities which were prehended, positively or negatively. We must push our analysis as far as possible, but in the last analysis only an educated guess is possible. The analysis offers no certitude.

Once the analysis is made of the physical prehension of the temporal actual entities which have contributed to the becoming experience, it is difficult to assume that these were the only contributing factors in the experience. There must be some other entities besides the temporal ones which contribute to this process. Whitehead designates this other type of entity as "eternal objects." Eternal objects are non-temporal. Since they are non-temporal, although able to contribute to the becoming experience of a temporal experience, it is necessary that the nature of an eternal object be twofold. On the one hand, the eternal object must in some non-temporal way exist within itself. On the other hand, the eternal object must possess some "relational essence" to temporal entities. Being temporal, an entity must prehend an eternal object in a different manner from that of physical prehension. Whitehead designates this process of prehending eternal objects as "conceptual prehension." As in the case of temporal actual entities, all eternal objects cannot be prehended in a positive manner for the becoming experience. It is necessary that the experience be conceptually selective, choosing those eternal objects which can contribute positively to the creation of a new actual entity.

In our analysis of an actual entity, we have the becoming experience acting as a subject, making positive and negative prehensions of temporal and non-temporal objects. Since this selective process occurs, there must be some force within the becoming experience which is responsible for this selective process. Whitehead designates this force as the "feeling" of the becoming experience. The becoming actual entity is a subject which feels. On the basis of this feeling, some objects are prehended positively while others are prehended negatively. The way in which a particular subject feels a particular objective datum is called the "subjective form." By including some objects and excluding others, the feeling subject expresses "subjective aim." In other words the feeling contributes a directive purpose to the becoming experience. Because of the subjective aim, the experience becomes what it is instead of what it might have been. Particular potentials become actual while other potentials are rejected.

When the feeling subject reaches its subjective aim, the satisfaction of the actual entity occurs. In other words, the becoming actual entity has reached its "concrescence." This is the process of the coming together into a unity of the different parts of the experience. When the concrescence-satisfaction stage has occurred, the experience is no longer in the process of becoming but now actually exists as a new form in the universe. The working together of these different factors of a becoming experience make possible a new actual entity. That these factors do work together is understood by Whitehead as showing that "novelty" has come into the process of becoming. To say that novelty has occurred is another way of saying that this particular novel actual entity has become and now exists as a new form in the world.

As we consider the actual entity under analysis, it is obvious that it does not exist in its state of concrescence because at this time it is an object of our consideration. Whitehead asserts that a temporal entity perishes after it has reached its concrescence-satisfaction; it enters into a state of "objective immortality." The actual entity no longer functions solely as a subject of feeling; now it is an object of other feeling subjects. As an object, the subject of the actual entity is transformed into a "superject."

This is the doctrine of the emergent unity of the superject. An actual entity is to be conceived both as a subject presiding over its own immediacy of becoming, and a superject which is the atomic creature exercising its function of objective immortality. It has become a "being;" and it be-

longs to the nature of every "being" that
it is a potential for every "becoming."126

How does Whitehead's doctrine of God fit into our analysis
of this particular actual entity? In our analysis, there are
three factors which are difficult to account for completely. The
first concerns the non-temporal entities called eternal objects.
Since only a few eternal objects can be positively prehended in
a particular conceptual process, what happens to these eternal
objects as potentials when they are not being included in the
becoming of an experience? These eternal objects are retained
by the Primordial Nature of God as this nature makes a conceptual valuation of the entire multiplicity of eternal objects.
Since these eternal objects are what they are according to
their own nature, they are retained or sustained by God but
are not conditioned in this process. Thus, the Primordial
Nature of God is necessary for the functioning of eternal objects. The second factor deals with the state of objective
immortality. It seems logical to assume that every actual entity
which has occurred cannot always be serving as an object in
the process of another becoming. What happens to these actual
entities which perish? Whitehead believes that in his Consequent Nature, God physically prehends all the actual entites in
the universe. In other words, God saves perishing actual entities in this aspect of nature. God is necessary for the retention or sustaining, not only of the non-temporal entities,
but also of the temporal actual entities which have become objectively immortal. The third factor deals with Whitehead's
metaphysical presupposition that there is an upward trend in
the evolving universe. If there is an upward trend, then
there must be some force operating within the universe that
bears some responsibility for this trend. Since creativity is
related both to the upward trend and the destruction which
occurs, it cannot be that force which is solely responsible for
the upward trend. Whitehead asserts that there is a Superjective Nature of God which acts as the force working to bring
about good or harmony in the universe instead of evil or destruction. Each actual entity in a state of objective immortality, as well as each eternal object, is used by this aspect of
the nature of God to bring about the upward trend. Since
God sustains all actual entities, God is potentially able to affect
directly each becoming experience in favor of the upward
trend. This aspect of God's nature is balanced by the fact
that each feeling subject is free to choose those actual entities
it so desires to contribute to its becoming. God has the power
to work for harmony, while at the same time this power is
limited by the freedom of each becoming experience. In essence, God is necessary for the entire process of becomings of
experience; yet, because of the freedom of each subject, God
cannot dictate the outcome of the becoming process. God is

all-inclusive; God saves, but God is relative due to the freedom of each subject.

How does our analysis conform to Whitehead's method? According to the method, we have started with man in the actual world having experiences. In an attempt to understand a particular experience, the analysis begins from a particular area of human interest, which for this analysis would be the philosophical area. Based on Whitehead's philosophical presuppositions, our observation has been guided by a "working hypothesis." It has been assumed that actual entities are the only real things that exist and that the reason for all things is to be found in the composite nature of definite actual entities. We have not dealt only with the obvious premises but have sought the more important premises that are not obvious in the experience. Language has been used carefully. We have tested our terms to be sure that they are the most descriptive for that which we mean to convey. Having made our descriptive analysis of the process of this actual entity and having considered the nexus of this actual entity, it is necessary to develop a philosophical generalization from this analysis. It is asserted that every temporal actual entity goes through a process of becoming, emerging as a new form in the world, and continuing to exist in a state of objective immortality as objects for other becoming actual entities. According to the method, our next function would be to test this generalization from the perspective of other areas of human interest. If this generalization is found from these other perspectives to be coherent, logical, applicable and adequate, it then is postulated as a universal or tentative ultimate principle. This tentative ultimate principle becomes part of the total metaphysical scheme which is used to consider the major philosophical problems.

VI

Evaluation

This evaluation will be made from two perspectives. The first will be an evaluation of aspects of the method in practice as presented in the brief sketch of the metaphysical scheme. The second evaluation will deal with the method in general.

It is basic to Whitehead's view that experience cannot be confined to human or conscious beings. Everything which constitutes human experience is to be found in the natural world, and vice versa. On the basis of this presupposition, Whitehead is able to develop his theory of "feeling" and his theory of a "moral order." In the coming together of every actual entity, the basic element is the fact that the subject feels. Granted that Whitehead is trying to form a general description which attributes qualities and functions to non-conscious things in ways not commonly done; there seems to be little support from non-speculative disciplines for non-conscious entities displaying the qualities of conscious entities. Unless there is some way of verifying this function of non-conscious entities, it seems difficult at this point to state that his scheme is "applicable" and "adequate." The same issue arises in connection with the idea of a moral order functioning within the Universe. Whitehead rejects the view that this moral order can be supported by the theory of evolution based on the doctrine of the survivial of the fittest. The judgment that there is an upward trend or a moral order is a human judgment, based on our conscious faculty. It is not only difficult to support the view of a non-conscious temporal subject with a faculty of feeling; it is just as difficult to support the view that a non-conscious entity can make evaluations about or participate in a moral order. Unless there is some way of verifying that non-conscious temporal entities can function in such a way as to support moral evaluations, this generalization cannot be supported by the requirements established in the method.

The docrtine of the process of an actual entity and the doctrine of objective immortality raise real difficulties. The basic force making possible the process of an actual entity is the creativity of the Universe. At the same time the feeling subject, taking into account the data from efficient and final causes, creates the concrescence of the actual entity. This dual creative process is an attempt to escape the trap of determinisn, but by retaining this dual factor an actual or at least potential contradiction exists. Since creativity is the basic force, it would seem that the actual entity creates itself within the limits made possible by creativity. In one sense Whitehead would affirm this limitation, while at the same time he would want to say that the subject creates itself and that to deny it this creative function is to deny it its freedom.

Another way of dealing with this issue is by considering the doctrine of relativity. Since creativity is not an actual entity, Whitehead does not deal with the question whether creativity is relative. All becoming, temporal actual entities are relative, and all non-temporal actual entities are relative. If everything is relative, it would appear that the theory of relativity itself is logically destroyed. Whitehead supports his relative view by retaining the state of satisfaction, the unity of the actual entity, as the one non-relative thing. The unity of concrescence is not relative at that instance. It might be possible to deal with the problem of creation by saying that the non-relative concrescence creates itself at the instant of its being non-relative.

Part of the doctrine of an actual entity is that it is continuous. The doctrine of objective immortality is supposed to describe how the continuous state occurs. It seems a linguistic contradiction to say that an actual entity "perishes" and continues at the same time.127 Objective immortality seems to imply that the real actual entity does not continue, but that the potential of the actual entity for other entities continues. If only the potential of the actual entity continues, then it seems false to say that objective immortality supports the doctrine of the continuousness of an actual entity. This would mean that there is "real" discontinuity and "potential" continuity. So long as there remains this element of discontinuity in the cosmology, it would be necessary to deal with the issue whether the continuous or discontinuous factor is ontologically fundamental. Whitehead uses God's Consequent Nature to save the "potential" continuousness. Why could not this "potential" continue in the physical prehensions of temporal becoming actual entities? Let us accept Whitehead's assertion that all objective actual entities are not at all times serving as data in the physical prehensions of temporal becoming entities. It then follows that the continuousness would be broken and the potential of the actual entity lost, if the continuousness is dependent upon the constant physical prehension of at least one becoming entity. It seems logical to assume his doctrine of God in order to have some force which sustains these potentials when they are not being realized. The question must be raised, however, whether God is used as a deus ex machina to support this retention. We have no way of supporting the thesis that these potentials exist even when they are not being actualized in a prehension. It is possible to assume that they do exist, but there is no way of supporting this assumption. Assuming that they do not exist apart from being prehended, it would seem logical to state that Whitehead has developed this function of God to support his theory that actual entities are continuous, although there remains the more basic problem whether there is actual continuity if only the "potential" of the actual entity continues.

If Whitehead is to overcome the limitations of the Newtonian view, it is necessary that the actual entity continue. If discontinuity is ultimate, there is no escape from the atomic-mechanical view to the view which concentrates on the idea of organism. The philosophy of organism overcomes the Newtonian view by the doctrine of extensive continuum. In his earlier philosophy of science Whitehead had handled this problem by emphasising relational continuity or the interdependence of things, thus staying within the limitations of efficient causes. In the metaphysical period, he shifts his emphasis to teleological or final causes, emphasising subjective aim or feeling. Potentialities are involved in both the mechanical and the teleological views. In the former the present is conditioned by the past, or in some way the past begets the present. In the latter case, the efficient causes are not rejected, but the emphasis is given to the future. The subjective aim is more concerned with what can arise out of the future than with the effects of the past. It is important to Whitehead that his view of futuristic process should be kept in proper tension with the idea of the efficient contributing factors, in order that the true perspective, recognizing both efficient and final causes, should not be distorted. God, in his Primordial, Consequent and Superjective natures, exerts strong directional influence upon the becoming process and its final actualization, and consequently Whitehead's view has a dominant futuristic orientation. Because of the dominant role of God in the becoming process, Whitehead does not seem to be able to keep an adequate tension between efficient and final causes. Since it is also questionable whether non-speculative and non-theological disciplines would agree that the becoming process is influenced to this great degree by final causes,128 one cannot help but wonder whether on this point Whitehead's view is influenced more by the teleological perspective in the history of Christian thought than by his scientific background.

It is questionable whether Whitehead develops adequately his doctrine of eternal objects. Eternal objects are non-temporal, secondary types of entities in the universe which are conceptually prehended by the feeling subject of a becoming experience. It is Whitehead's view that physical prehensions

67

only account for repetition and that repetition cannot account for the coming into being of a really new actual entity. Since these new things do become, it is necessary to account for them. It is asserted that eternal objects actualized in experience are necessary for novelty. Within Whitehead's system, the doctrine of eternal objects is necessary in order that novelty should occur. From one view, something non-temporal is to be considered supernatural. If emphasis is given to the supernatural realm of things, then the temporal realm is less real, and vice versa. The problem arises, however, whether eternal objects are real things in relation to the actual entities. Charles W. Morris points out that "since a conceptual prehension is a prehension of eternal objects, the whole theory of mind depends upon the validity of the notion of eternal objects."129   On the basis of at least one understanding of Whitehead's "ontological principle," it would seem that eternal objects have no reality except in relation to an actual entity which prehends them.

> The "ontological principle," at least in one of its meanings, is an unequivocal expression of the view that eternal objects, taken by themselves are nothing. For the ontological principle states that only actual occasions are real. . . .Hence it would seem perfectly clear that eternal objects are simply aspects of the actual occasions exemplifying them, and have no reality by themselves.130

These eternal objects are not always being conceptually prehended by temporal actual entities, but Whitehead maintains that they are being prehended by God in his Primordial nature. In this nature God is not conscious. It is questionable whether a non-conscious actual entity can conceptually prehend, especially in view of the fact that Whitehead goes to great length to transfer some form of feelings to actual occasions (which often are not considered to have feelings) in order that they may perform the conceptual prehension necessary for their becoming process. One seems led to agree with Charles Hartshorne that Whitehead has not developed adequately his doctrine of eternal objects.

> An obscure, if not definitely erroneous, feature of Whitehead's view is his notion of eternal objects. That these are legitimately distinguished from ordinary universals or essences is I believe a point well taken, but one which is by no means consistently carried out.131

A question will be raised concerning the doctrine of God in relation to the problem of evil, and fuller consideration will be given to this doctrine in the second part of our evaluation. Basically Whitehead is asserting that God is the ultimate ordering force for good in the universe. His other descriptions of God's nature are based on this. From Whitehead's perspective, God is never a complete actual entity, in the sense that he always includes within his nature other actual entities as they become objectively immortal. Since God is never complete, he never perishes; in this sense God is eternal. Eternal objects and objectively immortal actual entities also never perish within the nature of God. Whitehead is very careful in his doctrine of God that God is not responsible for evil or disharmony. The doctrine of objective immortality means that evil, as well as good, continues, being sustained within God's nature. It is part of God's nature to present these objectively immortal actualities to other becoming experiences as data. Some of these potentials, with their evil elements, are made actual in the becoming experience. This means that the good in becoming experience is less valuable than it might have been, if the past evil had been less evil. Since God sustains the past evil and is responsible in some way for presenting it to becoming actual entities, to some degree God may be responsible for the fostering of evil. Whitehead tries to overcome this difficulty by asserting that God includes past evil within his purpose for future good, but it is not clear that God totally transforms past evil into good. This may or may not be an adequate description of the way in which God functions in relation to evil, but it is questionable whether Whitehead's theory completely relieves God of all responsibility for evil.

It was stated previously that Whitehead's method applied metaphysically was designed to deal with three philosophical problems: (1) the one and the many, (2) efficient and final causes, and (3) permanence and change. His description of a becoming actual entity and his description of God explain how the one includes the many within its nature. The problem arises how God, the one, in his non-conscious Primordial nature is able conceptually to prehend eternal objects, and this raises the question whether the one is able to include this aspect of the many within its nature. Another issue is whether Whitehead gives adequate consideration both to efficient and to final causes. Because his emphasis upon process has a dominant futuristic orientation, it appears that the importance of efficient causes is minimized. It is also questionable whether the issue of permanence and change is satisfactorily handled. In the state of objective immortality, the essential objective "potentiality" of the perished actual entity is retained within God's Consequent nature, but the actual entity in its state of "actuality" perishes and is not retained. Attempting a theological analogy, we might say that God saves the "soul" of the perished actual entity, but that there is no "resurrection of the body." If only the continuity of "potentiality" is necessary and not of "actuality," then Whitehead's description fulfills its purpose from the perspective of coherence.

It must be remembered that Whitehead does not claim that his scheme is an absolute metaphysical description. On the basis of the most inclusive scientific information and on the basis of his insights into philosophical problems, he has attempted to develop a metaphysical scheme that will deal with the issue while being true to scientific data. There will always be limitations in any system which is not an absolute, but the greatness of Whitehead's attempt is that he realized basic problems and tried to deal with them. We should keep his limitations in view, but our primary emphasis should be on accepting the challenge offered by his insights to continue the metaphysical search. We can learn from his mistakes, but more importantly we can build on the spirit of his metaphysical attempt.

Whitehead's method is a method of speculative philosophy. Its value is that it calls man to take seriously today his responsibility to understand as much as possible about existence. The open-endedness of his method is important because the method itself includes the transcending of methods. "The speculative reason is in its essence untrammelled by method. Its function is to pierce into general reason beyond limited reason, to understand all methods as coordinated in a nature of things only to be grasped by transcending all method."132 Whitehead's method must be judged by its intention, namely to overcome the narrowness of separate perspectives and to develop an understanding of existence which takes into account all areas of human concern.

Whitehead's method is important to religion and theology. Indeed his method implies the religious spirit because it takes into account the total man. All religions have in their own way claimed some mystical insights. One of the great dangers of mystical knowledge is that it becomes dogmatic and in this way serves to limit man's total understanding. The purpose of Whitehead's method is to develop a philosophy which will take into account these mystical insights while at the same time refusing to allow them to become fixed and inflexible. He clearly points this out in a conversation with W. E. Hocking: "If you like to phrase it so, philosophy is mystical. For mysticism is direct insight into depths as yet unknown. But the purpose of philosophy is to rationalize mysticism."133 His method offers a bridge between religion and other disciplines. Whitehead asserts the essential importance of religion and calls upon reli-

70

gion and theology to take seriously their responsibility to relate their insights to the whole man and the entire range of his
knowledge.

VII

Doctrine of God

"Creativity" is the basic force of the Universe. God did not create the Universe out of nothing. The Universe is given with its force of creativity. "The true metaphysical position is that God is the aboriginal instance of this creativity, and is therefore the aboriginal condition which qualifies its action."134 Creativity is the basic universal force, but God is that force which gives unity and direction to the universal process. God is limited by the creative force, but at the same time God conditions creativity. "He is the principle of concretion -- the principle whereby there is initiated a definite outcome from a situation otherwise riddled with ambiguity."135

Whitehead considers God from the perspective of three natures. "(1) The 'primordial nature' of God is the concrescence of an unity of conceptual feelings, including among their data all eternal objects. (2) The 'consequent nature' of God is the physical prehension by God of the actualities of the evolving universe. (3) The 'superjective' nature of God is the character of the pragmatic value of his specific satisfaction qualifying the transcendent creativity in the various temporal instances."136 With these three natures in view, we shall consider his doctrine of God from three perspectives. The first point concerns the way in which God affects the world. The second will be concerned with the way in which the world affects God. The third will take account of the religious qualities Whitehead attributes to God. How God affects the world and vice versa, will be considered in terms of the threefold nature of God outlined above.

In his Primordial Nature, God affects the world as "the Unmoved Mover" of the Universe. There is "an underlying eternal energy in whose nature there stands an envisagement of the realm of all eternal objects."137 Eternal objects receive a unity of togetherness in God, and are sustained by this first nature of God. The eternal objects are non-temporal forms of subjective aim for the Universe. God presents selected eternal objects to a becoming experience. In this way God is responsible for the initial subjective aim of the becoming temporal actual entity. By this action the temporal is joined with the eternal.

> The things which are temporal arise
> by their participation in the things which
> are eternal. The two sets are mediated by
> a thing which combines the actuality of
> what is temporal with the timelessness of
> what is potential. This final entity is the
> divine element in the world, by which the
> barren inefficient disjunction of abstract
> potentialities obtains primordially the effi-
> cient conjunction of ideal realization.138

The becoming experience is not responsible for its initial subjective aim, although in its freedom it is responsible for the
manner in which the subjective aim is fulfilled. Whitehead
asserts that novelty has occurred in the Universe when an actual entity has become. The actual entity conceptually prehends from God its subjective aim; in this way God is responsible for the "novelty" in the Universe.

> Those of God's feelings which are
> positively prehended are those with some
> compatibility of contrast, or of identity,
> with physical feelings transmitted from the
> temporal world. . . .Apart from the inter-
> vention of God, there could be nothing new
> in the world, and no order in the world. .
> . .The novel hybrid feelings derived from
> God, with the derivative sympathetic con-
> ceptual valuations, are the foundations of
> progress.139

In his Primordial Nature, God is infinite, containing all
the possibilities for the universal process. But God is neither
conscious nor does he have feeling in this nature. If God did
have feeling and consciousness, he could be held responsible
for the evil that develops on the basis of the subjective aims
which he supplies to the becoming experiences.

> We must ascribe to him neither fulness
> of feeling, nor consciouness. He is the
> unconditioned actuality of conceptual feel-
> ing at the base of things; so that, by rea-
> son of this primordial actuality, there is
> an order in the relevance of eternal objects
> to the process of creation. His unity of
> conceptual operations is a free creative
> act, untrammelled by reference to any par-
> ticular course of things. It is deflected
> neither by love, nor by hatred, for what
> in fact comes to pass. The particularities

of the actual world presuppose it; while it
merely presupposes the general metaphysical character of creative advance, of which
it is the primordial exemplification. The
primordial nature of God is the acquire-
ment by creativity of a primordial char-
acter.140

It is the actions of God that make possible the order or
upward trend in the universe. Creativity receives a definite
character by the conditioning force of God. In his Primordial
Nature, God transcends the temporal order by the unity he affords eternal objects, but more important is God's immanence
in the temporal order by his presentation to the becoming actual entity of its initial subjective aim. It is by God's action
that there is order and novelty in the Universe. "The immanence of God gives reason for the belief that pure chaos is intrinsically impossible."141

God affects the actual entities of the world in a saving
manner in his Consequent Nature. God as the principle of
concretion in the Universe is both the beginning and the end
of the process. He is the beginning in his Primordial Nature.
"He is not the beginning in the sense of being in the past of
all members. He is the presupposed actuality of conceptual
operation in unison of becoming with every other creative
act."142 When the actual entity "perishes," it becomes objectively immortal in the Consequent Nature of God. God saves
the actual entity by taking it into his own nature. God's gift
of subjective aim is the beginning of a becoming actual entity,
and the end of the process is salvation in the nature of God.
In this nature God feels and is conscious, and it is because of
these qualities that he is able to save the actual entities. God
is an eternal process in that he takes unto himself all actual
entities which have perished and in that it is inherent within
his nature that he will always perform this function of salvation. Whitehead asserts that God shows infinite patience and
love in his Consequent Nature.

In the Superjective Nature, God affects the world by ac-
tively working to bring about the "upward trend" in the temporal world. By working for the upward trend, God attempts
to save the entire creative process, whereas in his Consequent
Nature God offers salvation only to individual actual entities.
He is conscious and feels in this nature. In this state God has
his satisfaction, though it is never complete. He is responsible
not only for the subjective aim of the becoming experience; God
is also responsible for the objectively immortal data of which
becoming experience makes use.143 God, by his infinite wisdom, tries to convey the subjective aim and the objective data

in such a way as to qualify the upward trend of the temporal world. He takes the good and evil objective data and tries to shape them in such a way that good comes from that which is evil. In his Consequent Nature, God saves the actual entities of the temporal world. In his Superjective Nature, he works to save the entire creative process of the Universe.

God, the three-in-one, transcends the world while at the same time being immanent in the world. He transcends the world on the same basis that each actual entity transcends every other actual entity. God is immanent in the world in that (1) he is responsible for both the subjective aim and objective data used by the becoming experience, (2) he saves the perished actual entity by making possible the extensive continuum, and (3) he works to save the universal process by the upward trend in the temporal world.

It is not so clear how the world affects God. Under the idea of the Primordial Nature of God, Whitehead asserts that God sustains the potentials which can only be made actual in the temporal world. If the temporal entities were not dependent upon God for their subjective aims, then God's Primordial Nature would not be relevant to the temporal world. God's Consequent Nature and Superjective Nature are more directly affected by the world. In these natures, God functions as a feeling and conscious becoming actual entity. The temporal objective entities provide God with data. God could not be an actual entity in process without the increase made possible by the prehension of the objective data of the world. In other words, God's satisfaction is affected by the world. The satisfaction of every actual entity is relatively dependent upon the data it prehends. Since God is an actual entity, his satisfaction is relatively dependent upon the temporal data which he prehends.

> Thus by reason of the relativity of all things, there is a reaction of the world on God. The completion of God's nature into a fulness of physical feeling is derived from the objectification of the world in God. He shares with every new creation its actual world; and the concrescent creature is objectified in God as a novel element in God's objectification of that actual world. This prehension into God of each creature is directed with the subjective aim, and clothed with the subjective form, wholly derivative from his all-inclusive primordial valuation, God's conceptual nature is unchanged, by reason of its final com-

pleteness. But his derivative nature is consequent upon the creative advance of the world.144

Whitehead has developed his metaphysical scheme in such a way that the world depends upon God for its completion, and God depends upon the world for his completion. Whitehead asserts this relative interdependence between God and the world in a group of antitheses:

> It is as true to say that God is permanent and the World fluent, as that the World is permanent and God is fluent.
> It is as true to say that God is one and the World many, as that the World is one and God many.
> It is as true to say that, in comparison with the World, God is actual eminently, as that, in comparison with God, the World is actual eminently.
> It is as true to say that the World is immanent in God, as that God is immanent in the World.
> It is as true to say that God transcends the World, as that the World transcends God.
> It is as true to say that God creates the World, as that the World creates God.
> God and the World are the contrasted opposites in terms of which Creativity achieves its supreme task of transforming disjoined multiplicity, with its diversities in opposition, into concrescent unity, with its diversities in contrast.145

The doctrine of God presented by Alfred North Whitehead is a metaphysical description of God, dependent upon and conforming to his metaphysical scheme. At the same time, this doctrine of God implies more than a metaphysical God; it describes a religious God. Whitehead's method requires that the contributions of religion be taken into account in his doctrine of God. Religion and theology are definite areas of human interest in which descriptive generalizations, especially dealing with God, must be tested. Whitehead does more than indicate the methodological necessity of taking religious insights seriously. All his metaphysical works deal in some way with the positive and negative contributions of religion to his metaphysical concern.

How does Whitehead's doctrine of God describe a religious God? Definite terms are used to describe God which traditionally have been used to express the religious qualities of God. In fact, the term "God" is a religious term; it has been used by philosophers, but it remains a religious term in content and emotion. Aristotle used the term "the Unmoved Mover" in his philosophical description of God. In the theology of the Middle Ages, this term acquired religious significance. Whitehead uses the term within the context of the Primordial Nature of God, and he retains the religious significance allowable within the context of his use. The three natures of God all assert that God is eternal and that he transcends the world. God is perfect in that he contains perfectly all the potentials for the world and perfect in the sense that he is perfecting the world. The term "omnipresent" and "omniscient" can be used to describe God, because on the one hand he affects all actual entities and on the other hand he displays his infinite wisdom as he works for the upward trend of the world.

The God described by Whitehead is an active savior God. He saves the world in two ways. In his Consequent Nature, he saves the actual entities of the world through the process of objective immortality. All temporal things perish, but they are saved in "everlastingness" with God.

> Throughout the perishing occasions in the life of each temporal Creature, the inward source of distaste or of refreshment, the judge arising out of the very nature of things, redeemer or goddess of mischief, is the transformation of Itself, everlasting in the Being of God. In this way, the insistent craving is justified -- the insistent craving that zest for existence be refreshed by the ever-present, unfading importance of our immediate actions, which perish and yet live for evermore.146

In his Superjective Nature, God saves the world by transforming the evil we do into the good which makes possible the upward trend of the world. God shows love, patience, wisdom in judgment. He suffers and finally triumphs. He shows love in that he cares enough to save every actual occasion, no matter how evil it may have been. Patience is shown in that he does not force us to conform in every way to his plan for the upward trend of the world. God shows infinite wisdom in the way that he judges the perished actual entities and conveys these data to becoming experiences in order that the upward trend will be sustained. He suffers in that his satisfaction shares all the suffering of our satisfaction. "This is the notion of redemption through suffering, which haunts the world."147 Man knows that God is a lover of man, his judge and his fellow-sufferer. The order of the universe as process informs us that there is a progressive upward trend in the world.148 We know that evil is part of our becoming experiences, but the upward trend informs us that God triumphs in his work to transform our evil into good. God is immanent in the world as he transforms it for his purpose of good, yet he transcends the world in that the evil of the world cannot limit ultimately the immanent purpose of God. In his Consequent and Superjective natures, God is a conscious feeling subject. He is God; God is person in the religious sense. He is the ground of all being who loves all, judges all, saves all in his suffering, and transforms all in his triumphant immanent presence.

VIII

View of Religion

The view of religion, as well as his view of education, is part of Whitehead's attempt to deal with the practical concerns of man. Metaphysical descriptions are of great value to man, but they do not fulfill their value unless they help meet the religious hunger of man. From his historical perspective, Whitehead tries to show how religious insights have developed, what their value is, and what their limitations are.

Religious insight begins when "our sense of the value of details for the totality dawns upon our consciousness. This is the intuition of holiness, the intuition of the sacred, which is at the foundation of all religion."[149] Man's environment conditions his external life, but this intuition of the sacred comes from the self-realization of existence made possible by the internal life. The history of religions shows that man goes through several stages before he reaches the final satisfaction of religion. At the same time all religion begins with the primary foundation of man's own solitariness and has as its goal "individual worth of character."

> Religion is what the individual does with his own solitariness. It runs through three stages, if it evolves to its final satisfaction. It is the transition from God the void to God the enemy, and from God the enemy to God the companion.
> Thus religion is solitariness; and if you are never solitary, you are never religious. . .what should emerge from religion is individual worth of character.[150]

Religion has been externally expressed in four ways in history: ritual, emotion, belief and rationalization. On the basis of common experiences and feelings, men develop ritual. If the emotions of the group become more defined, ritual is used as a means of expressing the emotions. Later beliefs are developed as verbal expressions of ritual and emotion. In the more primitive cultures, the myth is used for the expression of belief.[151]

81

The myth explains the purpose both
of the ritual and of the emotions. It is
the product of the vivid fancy of primitive
men in an unfathomed world. . .the myth
not only explains but reinforces the hidden
purpose of the ritual, which is emotion.152

As the cultural situation becomes more complex and the religion
expands beyond the narrow originating group, a process of
rationalization becomes necessary.

Rational religion is religion whose beliefs and rituals have been reorganized with
the aim of making it the central element in
a coherent ordering of life -- an ordering
which shall be coherent both in respect to
the elucidation of thought, and in respect
to the direction of conduct toward a uni-
fied purpose commanding ethical approval.
153

The rational religion tries to develop a metaphysical understanding of existence based on the finest insights offered by
man's emotions and expressions of emotions. If the new form
of religion places its emphasis upon the "companion God" who
makes possible a positive ethic, then religion serves humanity
as a main instrument for progress. When the rational attempt
does not move to the final satisfaction of religion, it remains
"the last refuge of human savagery."154 When religion fails
to reach its final goal, its inspiration comes to rest in dogmas
instead of the companion God. Dogmatic expression is necessary, but dogmas are always just bits of truth and never absolute expressions. "Religions commit suicide when they find
their inspirations in their dogmas."155

All religions can and should claim truth for their insights,
but they should never claim absolute truth. Even the highest
form of religion, the religion of the companion God, can never
claim progress in depth of insight into human existence.

Progress in truth -- truth of science
and truth of religion -- is mainly a progress in the framing of concepts, in dis-
carding artificial abstractions or partial
metaphors, and in evolving notions which
strike more deeply into the root of reality.
156

Religion is not primarily individual; it has the social responsibility to serve as the foundation for the unity of civiliza-

tion. When religion attempts to fulfill its "great social idea,"
it justifies its insights by supporting the progressive order of
the world.

> The religious insight is the grasp of
> this truth: That the order of the world,
> the depth of reality of the world, the
> value in its whole and in its parts, the
> beauty of the world, the zest of life, and
> the mastery of evil, are all bound together
> --not accidentally, but by reason of this
> truth: that the universe exhibits a crea-
> tivity with infinite freedom, and a realm of
> forms with infinite possibilities; but that
> this creativity and these forms are together
> impotent to achieve actuality apart from the
> complete ideal harmony, which is God.157

The religion of Jesus was a higher form of religion in that
he placed emphasis upon the companion God. The Jewish view
of God was that of an oriental despot. "The progress of religion is defined by the denunciation of gods."158   There was
progress in the Jewish religion in that they moved from many
gods to one god, but they never completely moved, in Whitehead's term, "from God the enemy to God the companion."159
The greatness of any valuable religion consists in its "interim
ethic," which was an absolute ethic for Jesus who believed that
the social order was about to be destroyed and God would
save.   This interim ethic enabled Jesus to move from the
Jewish enemy God to the companion God who would save the
world. "A gracious, simple mode of life, combined with a for-
tunate ignorance, endowed mankind with its most precious instrument of progress -- the impracticable ethics of Christianity."160   The ethic of Jesus became impracticable when the
truth of the myth was rationalized into an absolute dogma.
This rationalization process began in full force with Paul. He
began by whittling down the sense of infinitude in the religion
of Jesus into finite and limiting concepts. Paul placed an absolute emphasis on ideas like heaven and hell. The limiting
factors of dogma were made more complex with the development
of the Roman Catholic Church. At the same time, the Roman
Catholic Church preserved one great value of religion, its
aesthetic appeal in worship. "The Reformation was one of the
most colossal failures in history; it threw overboard what
makes the church tolerable and even gracious, namely, its
aesthetic appeal; but kept its barbarous theology."161   Within
the Protestant tradition, theology became the guiding light of
religion. There have been both value and disaster in the effect of theology. On the one hand, the effort of religion to
provide an adequate theology has kept it from complete noxious

superstition. On the other hand, the disaster of theology is that it has banished novelty, limiting the progressive order of the world. "This theological disaster is what I mean when I speak of the mischief which follows from banishing novelty, from trying to formulize your truth, from setting up to declare: 'This is all there is to be known on the subject, and discussion is closed.' "162 Within the Modern Period and more especially since the fall of the Newtonian view, the limitations of theology have placed Christianity in an acutely negative position. Religion has come to rely on an escape to terms which are no longer meaningful to the modern person, "terms either suited to the emotional reactions of bygone times or directed to excite modern emotional interest of non-religious character."163 It is the responsibility of theology in each age to disengage its spiritual message from the associations of a particular imagery. Not to accept this responsibility is to exhibit a lack of faith.164 Religion needs a new approach in its theology, which will presuppose a more adequate method. A clash of doctrine with other insights should not be a disaster for religion; it should be an opportunity. Religion, especially Christianity, will not regain its proper role until it can face change in the same, if not more positive, spirit as do the other areas of human interest.

> The great point to be kept in mind is that normally an advance in science will show that statements of various religious beliefs require some sort of modification. It may be that they have to be expanded or explained, or indeed entirely restated. If the religion is a sound expression of truth, this modification will only exhibit more adequately the exact point which is of importance. This process is a gain. . . . The progress of science must result in the unceasing modification of religious thought, to the great advantage of religion.165

The great problem today is that religion and science must learn to live together. The forces of science have become so dominant in man's life, that religion can no longer afford to operate as if the scientific insights did not exist. Man will live within a scientific world; at the same time it is necessary that man also live within the religious world. "When we consider what religion is for mankind, and what science is, it is no exaggeration to say that the future course of history depends upon the decision of this generation as to the relation between them."166 The job of theology is to combine its religious experience and aesthetic expression with the insights of science. If man's humanity is to be fulfilled in the progressive order of the universe, then religion must accept the responsibility to afford mankind his necessary essential novelty in a manner which is understandable and relevant. Not to accept this responsibilty is to deny man the vision which gives meaning to existence.

> Religion is the vision of something which stands beyond, behind, and within, the passing flux of immediate things; something which is real, and yet waiting to be realized; something which is a remote possibility, and yet the greatest of present facts; something that gives meaning to all that passes, and yet eludes apprehension; something whose possession is the final good, and yet is beyond all reach; something which is the ultimate ideal, and the hopeless quest. . . .The vision claims nothing but worship; and worship is a surrender to the claim of assimilation, urged with the motive force of mutual love. The vision never overrules. It is always there, and it has the power to love presenting the one purpose whose fulfillment is eternal harmony. . . .The power of God is the worship He inspires. That religion is strong which in its ritual and its modes of thought evokes an apprehension of the commanding vision. The worship of God is not a rule of safety--it is an adventure of the spirit, a flight after the unattainable. The death of religion comes with the repression of the high hopes of adventure.
> 167

IX

Evaluation and Comparison

In evaluating Whitehead's doctrine of God and his view of religion, it is necessary to keep two perspectives in mind. On the one hand, Whitehead does write from a religious concern. His conception of God is of a God who meets man's religious needs and who brings salvation through suffering. On the other hand, his doctrine of God, though religious in quality and content, is broader than the personal categories of religious thought. Whitehead is attempting to develop a metaphysical description, and his doctrine of God is an integral part of this attempt. To view his concept of God apart from its metaphysical framework is to do partial violation to his doctrine of God, even to its religious qualities. Henry Nelson Wieman offers a summary statement of the cosmic problems that faced Whitehead in his metaphysical description in general and especially in his doctrine of God.

> The universe is made up of units which are highly active, call them atoms or what you will. The activities of these units are highly independent, one of the other. There is nothing in the nature of these units to keep them from frustrating and destroying one another and producing a hopeless confusion. Yet as a matter of fact they do not fall into such confusion. Doubtless there is plenty of confusion and frustration, but at the same time there is a very high degree of order, of mutual adjustment and mutual support between all these seemingly diverse and relatively independent activities. How can we account for this mutual support and mutual adjustment? Whence does it come? It does not come from the atomic units. It cannot come from the higher organization of these units, such as animals and men and societies, for these latter should never have arisen if the microscopic units were not adjusted and organized sufficiently for these more complex bodies to arise. Whence then comes this mutual adjustment and order?168

Seeing this mutual adjustment and order in the universe, Whitehead starts with the description of "creativity" as the basic force in the universe. Creativity is not an actual entity, so Whitehead cannot empirically prove that it exists. It is rather a term which he postulates on the basis of general observation. God cannot be this foundation term, for God is an actual entity and to make him responsible for the creative force would be to make him responsible for evil as well as good. Since creativity is not an actual entity but an inherent force operating within the universe, creativity is not responsible for evil and good. The contrasting forces of order and disorder just exist. There is no creation of the universe ex nihilo, and therefore there is no one actual entity responsible for good and evil. Whitehead regards God as the aboriginal instance of creativity.169   Since in some way creativity is responsible for God and all other actual entities, it would seem logical to assume that even though creativity is not an actual entity, in some way it is partially responsible for the evil which develops. As pointed out before, it would seem that God is also responsible in some way for evil, since it is through his retention and making available of perished actual entities that evil is able to influence the becoming experiences. Whitehead's intention is to assume that evil exists, while at the same time he denies any actual entity or creativity to be responsible for this evil. At the point of the social nature of evil, his doctrine of creativity and of God are not completely relieved of the responsibility for evil. Since his doctrine of God is based on creativity, Whitehead is unable to offer any factual reason why God is as he is. Since actual entities are the only real things, it is difficult to derive his view of God based on the idea of creativity. Creativity as a force and not an actual entity cannot logically afford any insight into the nature of God or even into the possibility that there is a God. Whitehead's doctrine of God can only rest on an argument that reminds one of the old cosmological argument, reasoning from the contingency of the world to a transcendent necessary Being. He uses this basic argument, giving it a new slant by placing the emphasis on God's immanence in order to deal with the problem of evil. Since it is questionable whether this device takes care of the problem of evil, it is also questionable whether his line of argument transcends the limitations of the old cosmological arguments, as pointed out by Kant.170

The Primordial Nature of God is the most fully developed part of Whitehead's doctrine of God. As Wieman points out, Whitehead sees an ordering principle in the universal process, which cannot be accounted for by his doctrine of creativity. The Primordial Nature of God is described as a logical explanation of this ordering principle. So far as this nature of God is concerned, Whitehead remains fairly consistent with his method. From the discipline of physics, he sees an operation of the universe which he cannot explain by physical laws. A descriptive generalization is postulated and tested from the different areas of human interest. In light of Whitehead's analysis of the becoming process of an actual entity and his analysis of the history of ideas and religion, there seems to be little, if any, evidence to support the contention that there is a force of order operating within the universe. Also there seems little traditional theological justification for naming this function God. Since this ordering process is far from perfect, it might be just as logical to assume that it is built into the universal system as a possibility, with disorder as the other possibility. Upon this latter line of thought, order or disorder would be decided by the becoming actual entity within its limited environmental freedom. In his Primordial Nature, Whitehead asserts that God is not conscious, that he is static, free from error and ignorance. At the same time God contains within this nature all eternal objects, having a vision of their potentialities. If God is not conscious, it seems hard to conceive logically that he can also have a vision of the potentials of all the eternal objects. Without this vision, this nature of God would be little more than a computer machine of potentials. Whitehead also asserts that God is an actual entity, and we assume that this nature of God shares in God's actuality. Since no new eternal objects emerge for God to retain and since he is not conscious, it is difficult to understand how in this nature God is an actual entity. An actual entity must conform to the becoming process of the universe. God in his Primordial Nature does not conform to this definition since he statically retains all the eternal objects ever possible. If God is in this nature a static, non-actual entity without vision, it seems logical to assume that he is the complete transcendent Unmoved Mover, having no godly immanent relationship to the actual entities of the temporal world. It is also questionable whether God can be non-conscious in his Primordial Nature while at the same time he is conscious in his Consequent and Superjective natures. Even if granted that Whitehead is talking about functions which God performs, it remains difficult to understand how God can be both conscious and non-conscious. It would appear, at least from the discipline of theology, to be a contradiction to say that God is conscious and non-conscious.

Since God is conscious and performs dual salvatory functions in his Consequent and Superjective natures, it is possible to consider these natures together. It is interesting to note that Whitehead does not really develop his thought concerning this aspect of God until the final short chapter of Process and Reality.171 These functionings of God are necessary to his system, but they are not fully or adequately developed. This lack of development at such a crucial point is in itself a great limitation in Whitehead's writings. By not developing adequately these concepts, Whitehead is not true to his method. He neither develops these generalizations enough nor does he test them descriptively within the context of other disciplines, at least within the writings available. It seems logical to assume that these concepts have not been adequately tested in other areas of human interest because there seems little evidence from the perspectives of other disciplines to support the view that there is a non-temporal actual entity which suffers and saves the world. The amount of seemingly illogical disorder in the universe could support the view that there probably is not a suffering God trying to bring about order in the universe.

It would seem that Whitehead has gone beyond the scope of observation and reason, outlined in his method, and has developed from some other frame of reference these concepts of God. It is obvious that these functions of God are developed in order to deal with the problem of evil and to offer a hope of some type of salvation. Issues have already been raised concerning the question how a non-temporal actual entity can operate within a temporal world in order to bring about salvation. Wieman asserts that Whitehead has developed a cosmic consciousness to serve man's religious needs for a God that will conserve all and insure the inevitable growth of good in some realm beyond the evils of this world. "So in the face of the ultimate tragedy, Whitehead yields and builds a dome of glory and perfection above this world which we know by observation and reason."[172] Wieman is correct in his condemnation of Whitehead in that these concepts of God are not self-evident. At the same time, there is some justification for the view which Whitehead has developed. His method pointed out that it would be necessary to think of things in ways not normally considered. He is trying to develop a description that involves man's emotional reactions, as well as the data offered by the sciences. The suffering, saving God does speak to man's emotional needs, while at the same time this idea tries to be true to the scientific view. Whitehead asserts in the beginning that his descriptive generalizations must go beyond the narrower spheres of any discipline and include the total man. His doctrine of God is not final or complete, but it is successful because it does not violate the general theories of science while at the same time it tries to meet the religious needs of man. There is success also because his open-ended method keeps his doctrine of God open to new insights, thus calling man not to make his doctrine of God an absolute or a religious dogma.

Traditional Christian Theology would raise many points of disagreement with Whitehead's doctrine of God, as well as with his whole metaphysical scheme. For the sake of our limited purpose, we shall consider three general problems. The first point raised would be that Whitehead's God is not the infinite and eternal God of the Universe and Beyond but is rather a limited God within the Universe. Whitehead would not deny this attack upon his doctrine of God. He would accept this criticism, but at the same time he would assert that his doctrine of God conforms to the scientific insights about the Universe, with God being eternal within the Universe while being limited to the conditions of the Universe. Any other description of God would violate the metaphysical method and scientific data, and it would make God responsible for evil. In summary, Whitehead would reject the supernatural God on two counts. On the one hand, to talk of a supernatural God is nonsense, because there is no scientific reason to justify belief in such a God. On the other hand, he would say that a supernatural God would be responsible for evil and by definition could not be God. There are no logical reasons to assume such a supernatural God, and if there were such a God, he could not be God by definition.

In the second case, traditional Christian Theology would assert that Whitehead's God does not actually save because he does not save the individual. Too often Christian Theology groups Whitehead with Albert Einstein and other philosophical scientists. Of course these men share much in common, but a quotation from Einstein will show that Whitehead's thought is very different.

> Nobody, certainly, will deny that the idea of the existence of an omnipotent, just and omni-beneficent personal God is able to accord man solace, help, and guidance; also, by virtue of its simplicity the concept is accessible to the most undeveloped mind. But, on the other hand, there are decisive weaknesses attached to this idea in itself, which have been painfully felt since the beginning of history. For example, if this Being is omnipotent, then every occurrance, including every human action, every human thought, every human feeling and aspiration is also His work; how is it possible to think of holding men responsible for their deeds and thoughts before such an Almighty Being? In giving out punishment and rewards He would to a certain extent be passing judgement on Himself. How can this be combined with the goodness and righteousness ascribed to Him?173

Whitehead does present a God that in his relative way is an omni-beneficent personal God, giving to man solace, help and guidance. His God saves every actual entity and in doing this saves the world through his working for an upward order. Christian Theology would expect Whitehead to say that God saves more than the actual entities, that he saves the persons of each individual within his nature. With his scientific frame of reference, Whitehead talks about actual entities and not basically about personalities. A person is a collection of actual entities and is always in process. In one sense God saves the person because the actual entities are saved. In another sense God does not save the person, because the person as such has no unique existence in God's salvation. Whitehead asserts that the essence of life is to live fully. It is of the essence of God's nature to help each actual entity fulfill itself. Christian Theology sees the real meaning of life to be in a future life with God, and, therefore, places emphasis on a personal salvation. Whitehead would say that Christian Theology has misunderstood the essence of life, and therefore, its theological emphasis is incorrect.

The third attack would hold that Whitehead's God is not the or a personal God.174 If, by definition, a personal God is such a God who is conscious and responds or relates himself to man through his conscious qualities, then Whitehead's God is a personal God. If one reads carefully the last chapter of Process and Reality, it seems almost absurd to suppose that Whitehead's God is not personal. The pronoun He is used to refer to God, which in no way can be taken to be neuter. In his Consequent and Superjective Natures, God is conscious; he loves and suffers; his satisfaction is increased; and he works for an increase in the temporal order. God is personally good because he never thrusts a desire on an actual entity, while at the same time, he works with evil to cause good. Being personal, God is both efficient and final cause. Whitehead would assert that to be personal, God must be able to love and suffer; and to love and suffer means that a being is affected by that which causes him to suffer in his love. In other words to be a personal God, it is necessary that God be relative to the world, in a process of becoming, and open to change under the conditioning factors of the world. Whitehead would further assert that it is exactly at this point that Christian Theology strips God of his personal quality. Theology has asserted that God is absolute, perfect and complete, while at the same time loving and suffering. These opposing natures of God are called a paradox, but in reality they are nonsense because a personal God who loves and suffers cannot be absolute, perfect and complete. God is personal, as all actual entities are personal; but to be personal God must be relative, as all actual entities are relative.

92

An evaluation of Whitehead's view of religion must be considered from the perspective of his intention, which is to present a positive philosophy of religion. Traditional theology has often developed its religious insights from an exclusive view of God, which at times has presented man with a God who negates his other areas of human interest. Jesus presented, according to Whitehead, religious insights which were basically positive; man was to live in love because God loved him and had expressed this love. Whitehead, in the positive tradition of Jesus, attempts to present a positive doctrine of God and a positive view of religion. God, who loves and suffers, always works for the upward order. Whitehead's evaluation of traditional religion is based upon this positive concern. He starts by showing how religion has positively developed. In the light of this positive development, limitations of religious development are then evaluated. He concludes his consideration by a positive call upon religion to accept the responsibility of its faith to make its insights constantly relevant to the changing process.

Whitehead's view of the development of religion is presented from a dual perspective, concerning the role of religion for man. On the one hand, religion is what man does with his solitariness. On the other hand, religion is definitely social; a crucial issue for religion is the relation of the individual to the community. All religions, especially beyond the primitive stage, have tried to keep this tension between the individual and social nature of religion.

It is possible to make a comparison between Whitehead's four stages of religious development and the stages outlined in Whitehead's method. Consideration begins from the area of a particular human interest. This area is a discipline with which the investigator is familiar; the familiarity compares with the religious ritual. Hypotheses are presented as guides for consideration. An evaluation is made as to the best possible direction; this stage is similar to the emotional stage which develops from the ritual. On the basis of observation and evaluation, descriptive generalizations are presented. At this point qualities and functions are often attributed to things which they are normally not considered to have. A descriptive generalization is tested in other areas of human interest; and if found adequate, it is presented as a universal insight. This testing stage compares with the rationalization stage in religion. The universal metaphysical principles, reached by the open-ended method, are never to be asserted as absolutes. This metaphysical lack of certitude compares with Whitehead's assertion that the failure of rationalized religion comes when its insights are presented as absolute dogmas.

Whitehead's four stages of religious development and three stages of development in the insights concerning God can be illustrated from the Bible, as well as from other developments in history of religion. In the Old Testament, the four stages can be more fully seen. As the people of Israel come together from their different backgrounds, they bring with them different religious rituals. Over a period of time these rituals are consolidated and take on the emotional content of being God's chosen people. Myths develop, e.g., Red Sea deliverance, which show how God protects and saves his chosen people. Especially after the Exilic Period, the rationalization process takes hold. At this stage religious insights are formulated, not as myths, but as a legalistic structure for religion. The development of the idea of God cannot fully be seen in the Bible. The Bible is a religious account, and the concept of "God the void"175 preceded such religious development. The Old Testament presents God as the enemy and God as the enemy-companion. God is the enemy of all people, including his own, who do not obey his will. At the same time God is the companion of those who obey his commandments, especially his chosen people. By the time of the inter-testamental period, the stage is set for a greater emphasis upon God the companion. Jesus places primary, if not complete, emphasis upon God the companion. God loves; God saves the individual from his worldly cares to his heavenly kingdom. With the rationalization process of Paul, God the enemy partially returns, though the primary emphasis is still upon God the companion. God remains basically love, but now God chooses some to heaven and does not choose others. From Whitehead's perspective, Jesus presented the highest form of religious insights concerning the nature and function of God.

In Whitehead's evaluation of the development of the Christian religion from Paul to the nineteenth century, there are some interesting insights but at the same time some restricted appreciation. His evaluation does not do justice to the theological contributions presented by Paul. It is true that Paul does establish more rigid and absolute dogmas for belief and condemns those who disagree. At the same time Paul's primary emphasis is upon the companion God. He rejects legalistic religion and places great emphasis upon "the mind of Christ" as a norm for human beings. All his writings show extreme love and concern, even though he often admonishes the people.

The evaluation of the effects of the Reformation offers true but limited insights. It is an overstatement to say that Luther and Calvin rejected the aesthetic qualities of religion. It was a definite concern of Luther to develop worship in such a way that the people could more fully participate. This participation by the people was to be enriching educationally as well as aesthetically. An evaluation of Calvin's evening prayer service confirms its aesthetic quality. The service is a drama, showing how the religious faith developed from the Old Testament to the New. It is true that those who built upon the Reformation often developed services of worship that rejected or greatly limited aesthetic value. This lack of aesthetic quality has been especially true from the period of Protestant Scholasticism and represents a definite limitation in the quality of theology. The Protestant tradition has often developed its rationalized process to absolute dogmas, making it necessary to limit aesthetic features which could not assert these absolute qualities. The effect of the Reformation may have been the limitation or rejection of traditional aesthetic values in the Christian religion, but it is unfair to state that Luther and Calvin are primarily responsible.

Whitehead's evaluation of the importance of the contemporary relationship between religion and science is excellent. It is true that we live in a scientifically dominated age which makes it even more vital that religion should speak to man's total needs. Instead of being defensive in relation to science, religion must reinterpret its insights in order to meet man's emotional needs while not clashing with his intellectual growth. In order to do this religion must include all areas of human concern, including science, within its frame of reference.

The insights of Alfred North Whitehead are no final answer to those who try to find a more relevant way of interpreting religious faith within the contemporary situation. Whitehead would never make this claim. His method demands that his insights should never become final answers or dogmas. Religion is called upon, through his open-ended method, to seek continually new and more adequate ways of expressing the truths of the faith. A religious person in the scientific age often searches for better ways to understand the meanings of his faith and for more adequate ways of expressing these meanings. Our evaluations and comparisons have presented the possibility that Whitehead's method and religious insights may be of service in understanding the nature of reality and in better understanding and expressing one's faith in relation to this reality. Whitehead stated that his purpose was to develop a position of rationalized mysticism. On the basis of his method, he has presented us with a contemporary myth for understanding the nature of total reality, as well as for understanding our religious natures. Both the method and myth may help us to develop a more adequate theological method and a better understanding and expression of the meaning of the Religious Myth. We end with a quotation by Bernard Eugene Meland, giving testimony to the stimulating effect of Whitehead's method and religious insights for the searching person.

For beneath this talk about God heeding the claims of man, or being attentive to his predicament, is the matter of the nature of reality, the kind of world process in which man must pursue his destiny. On this matter, Whitehead has been most illuminating. He has spoken to the religious man's condition. He has called him from the lethargy of acquiescence to a static deity, and has urged him to join hands with a Creator. He has roused him from the pampering of his own ego, from the plight of self-pity and self-concern, to participation in an enterprise of vast proportion, wherein the drama of the earth's seasons, the perennial cycle of perishing and new growth, is given its cosmic setting. To grasp the significance of living and of growth in the midst of the earth's perishings, to assess man's impluse to praise life in the face of the tragic sense of life, this is to rise to the religious man's vision of things, and to be equal to demands which creativity and our creature role lay upon us. On this matter, Whitehead's thought has been particularly fruitful.176

FOOTNOTES

1 This division of interests is not shared by all students of Whitehead. cf., Rasvihary Das, The Philosophy of Whitehead. London: James Clarke & Co. Ltd., 1938, p. 12ff; M. H. Moore, "Mr. Whitehead's Philosophy," Philosophical Review, Vol. 40, p. 268ff; and R. G. Collingwood, The Idea of Nature. Oxford: The Clarendon Press, 1945, p. 176.

2 cf., A. N. Whitehead, Principles of Natural Knowledge. Cambridge: University Press, 1919, p. 12-13ff.

3 cf., A. N. Whitehead, The Principle of Relativity. Cambridge: University Press, 1922, p. 4.

4 cf., Ivor Leclerc, "Whitehead and the Problem of Extension," Journal of Philosophy, Vol. 58, p. 559.

5 A. N. Whitehead, The Concept of Nature. Cambridge: University Press, 1955, p. 59.

6 For differing views on the development of Whitehead's metaphysical position, cf., Ivor Leclerc, Whitehead's Metaphysics. London: George Allen & Unwin Ltd., 1958, p. 4ff.; Nathaniel Lawrence, "Deity in Whitehead's Philosophy," Journal of Philosophy, Vol. 58; and J. E. Menge, "Professor Whitehead's Philosophy," The Catholic World, 1932.

7 Ivor Leclerc, "Whitehead's Philosophy," Review of Metaphysics, Vol. II, p. 95.

8 cf., A. N. Whitehead, Process and Reality. New York: Macmillan Co., 1957, p. 95.

9 cf., A. H. Johnson, "Whitehead's Philosophy of History," Journal of the History of Ideas, Vol. 7.

10 A. N. Whitehead, Process and Reality, p. 6.

11 A. N. Whitehead, Adventures of Ideas. New York: New American Library, 1959, p. 235.

12 cf., W. N. Urban, "Elements of Unintelligibility in Whitehead's Metaphysics," Journal of Philosophy, Vol. 35, p. 622ff.

13 cf., A. N. Whitehead, <u>Process and Reality</u>, p. 16-17.

14 A. N. Whitehead, "Analysis of Meaning," <u>Science and Philosophy</u>. New York: Wisdom Library, 1948, p. 136. cf., A. N. Whitehead, <u>Dialogues of Alfred North Whitehead</u> (Recorded by Lucien Price). New York: New American Library, 1956, p. 325, 364.

15 A. N. Whitehead, <u>Process and Reality</u>, p. 17.

16 William Christian, <u>An Interpretation of Whitehead's Metaphysics</u>. New Haven: Yale University Press, 1959, p. 3.

17 A. N. Whitehead, <u>Process and Reality</u>, p. 37.

18 <u>Ibid.</u>, p. 70.

19 There is much general disagreement with Whitehead's interpretation of "process." cf., A. J. Reck, "Substance, Process, and Nature," <u>Journal of Philosophy</u>, Vol. 55, p. 722; R. B. Winn, "Whitehead's Concept of Process," <u>Journal of Philosophy</u>, Vol. 55, p. 713; and John W. Blyth, "On Mr. Hartshorne's Understanding of Whitehead's Philosophy," <u>Philosophical Review</u>, Vol. 46, p. 527.

20 A. N. Whitehead, <u>Process and Reality</u>, p. 337-8. cf., R. C. Whittemore, "The Metaphysics of Whitehead's Feeling," <u>Studies in Whitehead's Philosophy</u>. New Orleans: Tulane University, 1961, p. 112; and M. H. Moore, "Mr. Whitehead's Philosophy," <u>Philosophical Review</u>, Vol. 40, p. 275.

21 cf., Rasvihary Das, <u>The Philosophy of Whitehead</u>, p. 182; and H. N. Lee, "Causal Efficacy and Continuity in Whitehead's Philosophy," <u>Studies in Whitehead's Philosophy</u>, p. 68. Both men disagree with Whitehead's doctrine of objective immortality.

22 A. N. Whitehead, <u>Process and Reality</u>, p. 33.

23 cf., <u>Ibid.</u>, p. 46.

24 <u>Ibid.</u>, p. 134.

25 <u>Ibid.</u>, p. 135.

26 <u>Ibid.</u>, p. 47.

27 <u>Ibid.</u>, p. 67.

28 cf., A. N. Whitehead, Process and Reality, p. 63; Adventures of Ideas, p. 230; Science and the Modern World. New York: New American Library, 1959, p. 179.

29 cf., A. N. Whitehead, Adventures of Ideas, p. 105; and Process and Reality, p. 16.

30 cf., A. N. Whitehead. Process and Reality, p. 30.

31 A. N. Whitehead, Adventures of Ideas, p. 150.

32 cf., A. N. Whitehead, Dialogues of Alfred North Whitehead, p. 132.

33 cf., A. N. Whitehead, Science and the Modern World, p. 24.

34 cf., A. N. Whitehead, Adventures of Ideas, p. 120; and Function of Reason, p. 11. Princeton: Princeton University Press, 1929.

35 A. N. Whitehead, Science and the Modern World, p. 22.

36 Ibid., p. 179.

37 cf., A. N. Whitehead, Function of Reason, p. 34.

38 cf., A. N. Whitehead, Adventures of Ideas, p. 47.

39 cf., A. N. Whitehead, Modes of Thought. New York: Capricorn Books, 1958, p. 99ff.

40 cf., A. N. Whitehead, Process and Reality, p. 16; and Adventures of Ideas, p. 3.

41 A. N. Whitehead, Modes of Thought, p. 70-71.

42 Ibid., p. 205.

43 cf., A. N. Whitehead, Modes of Thought, p. 156; Function of Reason, p. 22ff; and Process and Reality, p. 182.

44 cf., A. N. Whitehead, Modes of Thought, p. 151.

45 cf., A. N. Whitehead, Process and Reality, p. 76.

46 Ibid., p. 95.

47 Ibid., p. 101.

48 Ibid., p. 103.

49 A. N. Whitehead, Adventures of Ideas, p. 273-4.

50 Ibid., p. 275.

51 Ibid., p. 279.

52 cf., Yale Review, Vol, 23. Cohen and Urban maintain that Whitehead has retained the more significant insights of traditional idealism. cf., M. R. Cohen, "An Adventurous Philosopher," Yale Review, Vol. 23, p. 174; and W. M. Urban, "Elements of Unintelligibility in Whitehead's Metaphysics," Journal of Philosophy, Vol. 35, p. 637.

53 A. N. Whitehead, Process and Reality, p. 4.

54 Ibid., p. 13.

55 A. N. Whitehead, "Study of the Past--Its Use and Danger," Science and Philosophy, p. 165.

56 cf., A. N. Whitehead, Adventures of Ideas, p. 22.

57 Ibid., p. 156.

58 A. N. Whitehead, Dialogues of Alfred North Whitehead, p. 280.

59 cf., A. N. Whitehead, Science and the Modern World, p. 185.

60 A. N. Whitehead, Adventures of Ideas, p. 145.

61 A. N. Whitehead, Modes of Thought, p. 66-67.

62 cf., Ibid., p. 22.

63 A. N. Whitehead, Function of Reason. p. 60.

64 Ibid., p. 32.

65 cf., A. N. Whitehead, Process and Reality, p. 12.

66 Ibid., p. 481.

67 Ibid., Chapter V.

68 For a fuller consideration of this point, cf., P. D. Wightman, "Whitehead's Empiricism," The Relevance of White-

head. London: George Allen & Unwin Ltd., 1961, p. 335-50.

69 cf., A. N. Whitehead, <u>Process and Reality</u>, Chapter V.

70 <u>Ibid</u>., p. 86.

71 <u>Ibid</u>., p. 88.

72 <u>Ibid</u>., p. 92.

73 <u>Ibid</u>., p. 84.

74 <u>Ibid</u>., p. 85.

75 <u>Ibid</u>., p. 91.

76 cf., <u>Ibid</u>., p. 81. Whitehead asserts that Hume actually repudiates this presupposition.

77 <u>Ibid</u>., p. 208.

78 cf., <u>Ibid</u>., p. 208.

79 cf., <u>Ibid</u>., p. 201.

80 cf., <u>Ibid</u>., p. 210.

81 <u>Ibid</u>., p. 182.

82 <u>Ibid</u>., p. 34.

83 <u>Ibid</u>., p. 212-3.

84 cf., <u>Ibid</u>., p. 213.

85 cf., <u>Ibid</u>., p. 215.

86 A. N. Whitehead, "Uniformity and Contingency," <u>Science and Philosophy</u>, p. 153-4.

87 It is important to note that when the terms "empirical" or "empiricism" are used they refer neither to the position of Locke nor of Hume but, rather, are to be considered within the context of this altered process character of empiricism.

88 A. N. Whitehead, <u>Modes of Thought</u>, p. 181-2; also cf., <u>Adventures of Ideas</u>, p. 279.

89 cf., A. N. Whitehead, <u>Adventures of Ideas</u>, p. 226.

90 cf., _Ibid._, p. 227.

91 A. N. Whitehead, _Modes of Thought_, p. 154.

92 A. N. Whitehead, _Process and Reality_, Chapter VIII.

93 cf., _Ibid._, p. 7.

94 cf., _Ibid._, p. 15.

95 _Ibid._, p. 5.

96 cf., A. N. Whitehead, _Function of Reason_, p. 14.

97 _Ibid._, p. 5.

98 _Ibid._, p. 15.

99 _Ibid._, p. 18.

100 A. N. Whitehead, _Process and Reality_ p. 6.

101 A. N. Whitehead, _Adventures of Ideas_, p. 243.

102 A. N. Whitehead, _Process and Reality_, p. 7.

103 _Ibid._, p. 7.

104 A. N. Whitehead, "Analysis of Meaning," _Science and Philosophy_, p. 138.

105 cf., A. N. Whitehead, "Remarks," _Philosophical Review_, Vol. 46. It is Whitehead's contention that you can start from any area of human interest with his method. "My own belief is that at the present the most fruitful, because the most neglected, starting point is that section of value-theory which we term aesthetics. Our enjoyment of the values of human art, or of natural beauty, our horror at the obvious vulgarities and defacements which force themselves upon us--all these modes of experience are sufficiently abstracted to relatively obvious. And yet evidently they disclose the very meaning of things." (p. 184-5) Though it is not our purpose to develop Whitehead's method in relation to his aesthetic views, it is important to note that he places great emphasis upon aesthetics. It is because every person is to some degree involved with aesthetic appreciation that Whitehead contends that his method is open to use by all.

106 A. N. Whitehead, _Adventures of Ideas_, p. 223.

107 A. N. Whitehead, Process and Reality, p. 8.

108 A. N. Whitehead, Modes of Thought, p. 101-2.

109 A. N. Whitehead, Process and Reality, p. 10.

110 Ibid., p. 13.

111 Ibid., p. 11.

112 Ibid., p. 11.

113 Ibid., p. 12.

114 A. N. Whitehead, Function of Reason, p. 68-9.

115 Ibid., p. 12.

116 cf., Justus Buchler, The Concept of Method. New York: Columbia University Press, 1961, p. 169-71.

117 A. N. Whitehead, Function of Reason, p. 31.

118 Ibid., p. 51.

119 Ibid., p. 64.

120 A. N. Whitehead, Process and Reality, p. 163.

121 Ibid., p. 474-5.

122 cf., Ibid., p. 28.

123 A. N. Whitehead, Modes of Thought, p. 206.

124 A. N. Whitehead, Process and Reality, p. 47.

125 Ibid., p. 483.

126 Ibid., p. 71.

127 cf., Rasvihary Das, The Philosophy of Whitehead, p. 182.

128 cf., D. J. Miller, "Whitehead's Extensive Continuum," Philosophy of Science, Vol. 13, p. 146ff.

129 C. W. Morris, "Mind in Process and Reality," Journal of Philosophy, Vol, 28, p. 126, cf., A. E. Taylor, "Dr. Whitehead's Philosophy of Religion," Dublin Review, Vol. 181, p. 31.

103

130 E. W. Hall, "Of What Use Are Whitehead's Eternal Objects?" Journal of Philosophy, Vol. 27, p. 37.

131 Charles Hartshorne, "On Some Criticisms of Whitehead's Philosophy," Philosophical Review, Vol. 44, p. 344.

132 A. N. Whitehead, Function of Reason, p. 51.

133 W. E. Hocking, "Whitehead As I Knew Him," Journal of Philosophy, Vol. 58, p. 516.

134 A. N. Whitehead, Process and Reality, p. 344.

135 Ibid., p. 523.

136 Ibid., p. 134-5.

137 A. N. Whitehead, Science and the Modern World, p. 99.

138 A. N. Whitehead, Process and Reality, p. 63-4.

139 Ibid., p. 377.

140 Ibid., p. 522.

141 Ibid., p. 169.

142 Ibid., p. 523.

143 cf., A. N. Whitehead, Modes of Thought, p. 140.

144 A. N. Whitehead, Process and Reality, p. 523-4.

145 Ibid., p. 528.

146 Ibid., p. 533.

147 Ibid., p. 531.

148 There are at least three possible reasons why Whitehead has this assurance concerning the upward trend. He rejects the doctrine of the survival of the fittest as offering this assurance. Based on his analysis of how actual entities become and how they develop into a nexus, he sees a movement or upward trend towards order instead of chaos. From his historical perspective, he considers the development of ideas to have been slow, but that there has been a definite upward trend in this development. From his evaluation of religion, which we will consider in the next section, he considers there to be an

upward trend in religion as man moves from God the void, to God the enemy, to God the companion. It is questionable whether Whitehead could have developed this assurance from a purely detached speculative position. Considering his religious concerns and the influence upon his life which he attributes to the Christian tradition, it seems reasonable to assume that this optimistic perspective is more related to his Christian heritage than to any detached evaluation.

149 A. N. Whitehead, Modes of Thought, p. 164.

150 A. N. Whitehead, Religion in the Making. New York: Macmillan Co., 1957, p. 16-17.

151 Whitehead realizes that this four stage development is not an absolute description. He points out that at times myth has preceded ritual, but in general he asserts his description to be historical.

152 A. N. Whitehead, Religion in the Making, p. 24-25.

153 Ibid., p. 31.

154 Ibid., p. 37.

155 Ibid., p. 144.

156 Ibid., p. 31.

157 Ibid., p. 119-20.

158 A. N. Whitehead, Adventures of Ideas, p. 18.

159 A. N. Whitehead, Religion in the Making, p. 24.

160 A. N. Whitehead, Adventures of Ideas, p. 25.

161 A. N. Whitehead, Dialogues of Alfred North Whitehead, p. 234.

162 Ibid., p. 173.

163 A. N. Whitehead, Adventures of Ideas, p. 170.

164 cf., Ibid., p. 169.

165 Ibid., p. 169.

166 A. N. Whitehead, Science and the Modern World, p. 162.

167 Ibid., p. 171-2.

168 H. N. Wieman and B. E. Meland, American Philosophies of Religion. Chicago: Willett, Clark & Co., 1936, p. 242.

169 It is not Whitehead's concern to describe either how creativity or God come into being. Creativity is presented as the basic, neutral force of the universe. In one sense God just seems to exist as that becoming actual entity which works to bring about the upward trend. In this sense God is not created. In another sense creativity seems to be responsible in some way for the existence and functioning of God; "God is the aboriginal instance of this creativity, and is therefore the aboriginal condition which qualifies its action" (Process and Reality, p. 344). Though Whitehead is not clear about how creativity is responsible for the existence of God, he seems to be saying two things: (1) creativity as a neutral force makes necessary the positive working of God; and (2) God works in such a way so as to bring about the actualization of the positive potentials made possible by creativity.

170 cf., Immanuel Kant, Critique of Pure Reason. Tr. Norman Kemp Smith. London: Macmillan, 1952, p. 284ff.

171 The background for this short chapter is to be found in Whitehead's statement on "God" in Science and the Modern World, p. 156-61.

172 H. N. Wieman and B. E. Meland, American Philosophies of Religion, p. 240.

173 Albert Einstein, "Science and Religion," Nature, Vol. 146, p. 606.

174 cf., William Temple, Nature, Man and God. London: Macmillan, 1935, p. 259; Charles Raven, Natural Religion and Christian Theology. Vol. II. Cambridge: University Press, 1953, p. 102-3; D. E. Trueblood, Philosophy of Religion. London: Rockliff, 1957, p. 265; and Victor Yarros, "Dr. Whitehead and Professor Mather," The Open Court, 1928, p. 735.

175 cf., A. N. Whitehead, Religion in the Making, p. 16-17.

176 B. E. Meland, "The Religious Availability of a Philosopher's God," Christendom, 1943, p. 501.